ABOUT CHINESE WOMEN

ABOUT CHINESE WOMEN

Julia Kristeva

**translated from the French by
Anita Barrows**

Marion Boyars
New York · London

Published in Paperback in 1986 by
Marion Boyars Publishers Inc
237 East 39th Street, New York, NY 10016

Marion Boyars Publishers Ltd
24 Lacy Road, London SW15 1NL

Reprinted in 1991, 1993

First British hardcover edition published by
Marion Boyars Publishers Ltd, 1977

Originally published in France in 1974 as *Des Chinoises* by
Edition des Femmes

© Editions des Femmes 1974
© This translation Marion Boyars Publishers Ltd 1977

Library of Congress Cataloging-in-Publication Data
Kristeva, Julia, 1941–
    About Chinese women.
    Translation of: Des Chinoises.
    Bibliography: p.
    1. Women—China—History. I. Title.
HQ1767.K7513 1986 305.4′2′0951 85–26935

British Library Cataloguing in Publication Data
Kristeva, Julia
    About Chinese women.
    1. Women—China—Social conditions
    2. Women—China—History
    I. Title II. Des Chinoises. *English*
    305.4′2′0951   HQ1767

ISBN 0–7145–2522–7 Paper

Printed in Great Britain by Itchen Printers Ltd, Southampton

Table of Contents

FROM THIS SIDE

CHINESE WOMEN

Note

These notes do not make up a book. They are simply a journal of facts and inquiries inspired by a trip I was able to take to the People's Republic of China in April/May 1974. They are intended to be read particularly in relation to the confusion provoked in our own society by the rise of this dark continent, whose silence and will insure its own cohesiveness. Women: the women of China. These notes have their origin in my attempt to deal with the tremendous and rapid changes in their condition. That, indeed, is the reason I wrote them in such haste.

Analytical sketches, bits of information, fleeting impressions: at times I've indulged in tangential discussions left open-ended, probing new regions of thought rather than providing answers. Neither a scholarly book nor a subjective essay. This work leaves something to be desired. I would have done well to have it reflect the prudence — if not the hesitation — that I believe is warranted by any attempt to speak about women as well as about China.

Many individual and collective studies helped me in my work. I have appended a bibliography of the most essential. I wish to thank in particular Mlle. Ling Pai Chin and Mme. Janin-Hua Changming for their advice and criticism.

The phonetic transcription of Chinese names, with the exception of a few well-known cities, follows the *pinyin* method currently used in China and in the teaching of Chinese to foreigners.

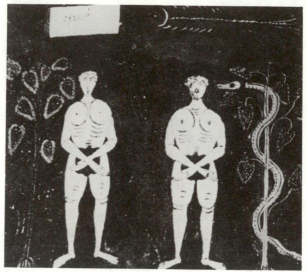

1. Adam, Eve and the serpent, by Beato de Liebana (around 711).
Pictures 1 and 2 represent two ideas of the relationship between the sexes.

2. Nügua and Fuxi: incestuous royal couple (impression from a relief by Pierre Han, 202 BC–220 AD).

FROM THIS SIDE

I

Who is Speaking?

Sitting here in front of the typewriter, trying to write about my experience in China, I am haunted by one scene in particular. It makes me hesitate at each touch of the keyboard; but it excites me as well. Not to lose sight of it; to make it transparent on every page: such are the stakes in the course that follows.

Forty kilometers from the former Chinese capital of Xi'an [the first capital of China after it was unified under the emperor Qin Shi Huangdi in the second century B.C., and the great capital of the Tang Dynasty (618-906)] is Huxian, the chief village of an agricultural region. The road we travel to get there is hot; the sun beats down on peasants in broad bamboo hats, on unsupervised children skipping about in quiet games, on a hearse drawn by some men while others, in two parallel lines alongside it, surround it with thin parallel poles carried across their shoulders. Everyone from the village is in the square where we are supposed to attend an exhibit of peasant painting in one of the nearby buildings. An enormous crowd is sitting in the sun: they wait for us wordlessly, perfectly still. Calm eyes, not even curious, but slightly amused or anxious: in any case, piercing, and certain of belonging to a community with which we will never have anything to do. They don't distinguish among us man or woman, blonde or brunette, this or that feature of face or body. As though they were discovering some weird and peculiar animals, harmless but insane. Unaggressive, but on the far side of the abyss of time and space. 'A species — what they see in us is a different species', says one of our

11

group. 'You are the first foreigners to visit the village', says the interpreter, always sensitive to the least of our tropisms. I don't feel like a foreigner, the way I do in Baghdad or New York. I feel like an ape, a martian, an *other*. Three hours later, when the gates of the exhibit are opened to let our cars pass through, they are still there, sitting in the sun — amused, or anxious? — calm, distant, piercing, silent, gently releasing us into our 'strangeness'.

Field anthropologists have certainly had such shocks: 'You are a different species.' But in China, the feeling of alienation seems to me even more important, because it is addressed to us by a society which has nothing exotic about it, no relation whatsoever to any 'primitive mentality'. On the contrary, it comes from what is called a 'modern nation', a nation with 'modern problems', in which even something that we may find irritating or archaic is easily identified: something not all that far from us, the regimes of Eastern Europe. So nothing disorienting there; even less so for me, who recognized my own pioneer komsomol childhood in the little red guards, and who owe my cheekbones to some Asian ancestor. The strangeness persists, then, through a highly developed civilization which enters without complexes into the modern world, and yet preserves a logic unique to itself that no exoticism can account for.

I think that one of the functions — if not the most important — of the Chinese Revolution today is to introduce this breach ('there are others') into our universalist conceptions of man and history. It's not worth the trouble to go to China if one insists on closing one's eyes to this breach. Obviously there are those who find a solution: they try to fill the abyss by rewriting a China *for* 'our people' (who may have some revolutionary or revisionist or liberal cause which will be strengthened by proving that the Chinese are *like* us, *against* us, or *to be ignored*); or else by creating a China *against* 'them' (against those who are deforming China by making it conform to 'their' ideology rather than 'ours'). To write 'for' or 'against': the old trick of a militant committed to maintaining his position. It can help, it can stifle: what is lost is the chance that the discovery of 'the other' may make us question ourselves about what, here and now, is new, scarcely audible, disturbing.

It is not my goal — and it is perhaps useless to try — to discover all those things which, in modern Chinese culture and society, determine the indefinable stare of the peasants of Huxian, who, in fact, did nothing but return the look I gave them without letting them see it, moulded as I am by universalist humanism, proletarian brotherhood, and (why not?) false colonial civility. I want to put into relief here one single aspect of that which creates the abyss between us and the villagers of Huxian: Chinese women, the Chinese family, their tradition, their present revolution. I make this choice for two reasons:

First, because the studies of specialists, my own impressions, and the most recent developments in the cutural revolution prove that, in ancient history but also throughout the history of Chinese socialism and up to the present, the role of women and, consequently, that of the family, have a particular quality in China which is unknown in the monotheistic West. To observe that particular aspect of China is, therefore, to try to understand what makes China unique: a focus which seeks to measure the distance that separates me from Huxian. No way at all to understand China if one is not sensitive to the women, to their condition, to their difference. Without that, there's no point even in being interested in China: one will know everything beforehand, and won't even hear the silence in Huxian Square; or, at best, if one hears it, one will be petrified by it, sickened, annoyed, separated forever from them; one will feel like forgetting them in order to forget at the same time the whole of China, or to understand it in one blow: easy.

Second, and perhaps especially, I make this choice because the *otherness* of China is invisible if the man or woman who speaks here, in the West, doesn't position him/herself some place where our capitalist monotheistic fabric is shredding, crumbling, decaying. But where? The class warfare, the new ideological and political mechanisms that have arisen since May '68 come to mind. Yes, certainly, especially when they don't mimic the reasoning of the capitalist system or the

13

classical parties they believe they're fighting. But do you know many who don't? We're left with the 'underground' — those who aren't yet organized, who in their impossible utopian 'dadaist' approach to politics provoke only laughter. And if the otherness, and therefore the novelty, of China were not visible except from there, because this underground, itself 'out of order' in our world, is its repressed content, the symptom of all that monotheistic capitalism has crushed in order to make itself everywhere identical and impermeable to crisis? The 'underground': women, young people, those who speak differently — artists, poets. . . . It is still essential that their anguish in the present community be more than just a disillusioned travesty of social bonds, or a sullen demand for a new social order. Living in the political system on the planet today, they must discover here and elsewhere that which is involved in an entirely different 'change of the tide' — an end to pre-history, dream and reality henceforth in continuous flux.

Women. We have the luck to be able to take advantage of a biological peculiarity to give a name to that which, in monotheistic capitalism, remains on this side of the threshold of repression, voice stilled, body mute, always foreign to the social order. A well-deserved luck, for, in fact, in the entire history of patrilineal or class-stratified societies, it is the lot of the feminine to assume the role of *waste*, or of the hidden work-force in the relationships of production and the language which defines them. But *a limited luck*, because others, men, since at least the end of the nineteenth century and in ever-increasing numbers in our time, realize that they have been the 'women' of the community: a misunderstanding, perhaps, that confuses the demands of the female sex (if you like), but which prevents a feminist 'we' from becoming a homogeneous 'secret society of females' and disseminates among others our own unnameable anxiety before all that escapes social restraint. A *luck* that will prove to have been *co-opted* if, after an initial phase — no doubt necessary — of searching for our identity, we lock ourselves up inside it: militant romantics of the final 'cause' to be thus revived, theologians of an inverted humanism rather than its iconoclasts.

14

Who is speaking, then, before the stare of the peasants at Huxian? Whoever on this side is fed up with being a 'dead woman' — Jewish mother, Christian virgin, Beatrice beautiful because defunct, voice without body, body without voice, silent anguish choking on the rhythms of words, the tones of sounds, the colours of images, but without words, without sounds, without images; outside time, outside knowledge, cut off forever from the rhythmic, colourful violent changes that streak sleep, skin, viscera: socialized, even revolutionary, but at the cost of the body; body crying, infatuating, but at the cost of time; cut-off, swallowed up; on the one hand, the aphasic pleasure of childbirth that imagines itself a participant in the cosmic cycles; on the other, *jouissance** under the symbolic weight of a law (paternal, familial, social, divine) of which she is the sacrificed support, bursting with glory on the condition that she submit to the denial, if not the murder, of the body. . . .

To relieve her of this weight, to x-ray it, to analyze it, is equivalent to a second Renaissance. Erasmus today would not write a praise of folly, but a critique of this negative term of the social entente, this eternal satire of the community, that is woman. If such is not the perspective, the women's movement is only good for establishing a ministry of women's affairs, i.e. an accelerated rationalization of capitalism. Which is not *nothing*; but even so. . . . In this round, will China be our Greece?

_A_few themes, then, a few names, chosen by accident of mood or desire, but dictated as well by the questions that my trip to China provoked in me: the sexual difference; the identification of the daughter with the paternal law; the atemporal and therefore apolitical appeal of polymorphic sexuality; suicide; the sacrifice of the other sex in a paternally dominated family where woman is 'the other race'; the totalitarianism which is the inevitable result of the denial of

---

*This word, for which there is no suitable English equivalent, is used in psychoanalytic contexts to mean the simultaneously organic and symbolic sexual pleasure of the speaking (human) subject.

this difference. Questions that the awakening of woman asks of our western society, questions that have a double interest for us here.

First, in that they show that *woman as such* does not exist. Either the term dissolves into as many individual cases, and, since the post-romantics already knew it (Rilke, for instance: 'Is it possible to say 'women', 'children', 'boys', and not suspect, for all one's culture, that for a long time now these words have had no plural, but rather an infinity of singulars?'), it's useless to cling to our belief in the latest community except to obtain the right to abortion and the pill. Or, the problems of women have no interest except inasmuch as they bring to an impasse the most serious problems of our type of society: how to live not only without God, but without man?

Secondly, to approach these problems beforehand will avoid dealing with them once we sense that we are encountering them in China; and we will have plenty of opportunities, when we see these girls who brandish pistols and paint-brushes, who liberate themselves from their husbands and fathers under the portrait of Mao, and leave their children, their calligraphy, their exploits in the field of production, science, or the current ideological campaign, as the sole evidence of their *jouissance*. It is more than the necessity to be brief that makes us avoid analyzing all this in China. Rather, it is a vigilance, call it ethical, that keeps us on our guard not to project onto the women of China thoughts which they may evoke but which, in fact, are the products of western experience and concern that alone. It's easy to ascribe innumerable reflections on the 'war between the sexes', the 'virgins of the word', 'timelessness' or 'suicide' to the silences that will occur throughout this journey in China and especially in the 'interviews' at the end: it will be a western vision. Nothing is less certain than 'the truth' about China according to some Viennese professor, or anyone else here in the West.

Refusing, therefore, to know more than they do; and refusing, as well, to endow them with a knowledge that would hold the answer to our own problems — let us first try to question a tradition that has defined us here for at least two thousand years. A quick sketch, a questionnaire, left open-ended.

The War Between the Sexes

The Lord God created the world and concluded alliances by *dividing* (karath) light from darkness, the waters of heaven from the waters of earth, creatures of the water from creatures of the air; by dividing the animals into species, and man from Himself, into His image. It's by dividing as well that he places them one facing the other: man and woman. Not without hesitation, though: for it is said at first that 'male and female created He them': but this original version is quickly corrected by the story of Adam's rib. Further on, the first female creature due to the hesitation where man and woman are not all that separate makes an ephemeral appearance in the form of the diabolical Lilith — emanation of Sodom and Gomorrah (Isaiah xxxiv-14). She comes up in several more or less heterodox exegeses, but not in the Bible itself.

Divided from man, made of that very thing which is missing in him, the Biblical woman will be wife, daughter, or sister, or all those things at once. She will rarely have a name. Her function is to assure procreation — the propagation of the race. But with the law of the community, with its political and religious unity, she has no direct relation: God, on the whole, speaks only to men. Which is not to say that woman doesn't know more about Him; indeed, it is she who knows the conditions, the material conditions so to speak — those of the body, of sex, of procreation — which permit the existence of the community, its permanence, and, therefore, man's dialogue with his God. Besides, is not the entire community the *Bride* of God? But woman's knowledge is corporeal, aspiring to pleasure rather than tribal unity: the forbidden fruit seduces the *eye* and the *mouth* of Eve. It is an informulable knowledge, an ironic common sense (Sarah, pregnant at 90, laughs at this bit of divine news); or else, when it serves social necessity, it's often in a roundabout way, after having transgressed the most ancient of laws, the incest taboo (Sarah declared the sister of Abraham; Lot's daughters sleeping in their father's bed).

Long before the establishment of the people of Israel, the Northern Semites worshipped maternal divinities. Even while such cults persisted, though, these farmers and shepherds began to isolate from them the principle of a male, paternal divinity and a pantheon in the image of the family (father-mother-son). But Judaism was founded beyond and by means of this tradition, when, about 2000 B.C., Egyptian refugees, nomads, highwaymen, and insurgent peasants banded together, it seems, without any common ethnic origin, without land, without a state, seeking at first to survive as an errant community. Jewish monotheism is undoubtedly rooted in this will toward community despite and because of all the unfavourable concrete circumstances: an abstract, nominal, symbolic community beyond individuals and their beliefs, but beyond their political organization as well. In fact, the Kingdom of David survived only a short time after its foundation in 1000 B.C., preceded by wars, followed by discord, finally becoming first the vassal, then the victim, of Babylonia. Devised to create a community, monotheism does not, however, accommodate itself to the political community that is the State; at its beginnings, it doesn't even help it. What it does is survive it and determine the direction it will take, long afterwards, through Christianity and up to various forms of modern secular and religious technocracies. But this is not the problem that concerns us here. Let us note only that by establishing itself as a symbolic principle of community — paternalistic, moralistic, beyond ethnic consideration, beliefs, and social loyalties, monotheism represses — along with paganism — the greater half of agrarian civilizations and their ideologies: women and mothers. The Syrian goddess who was

18

worshipped until the beginning of the Christian era in the Armenian city of Hieropolis-Menbidj, or the numerous sacrifices to Ishtar, survive the Biblical expurgation only in the traits of Deborah, the inspired warrior who accompanies the soldiers and sings their praise, or in the mouths of prophets who deplore the idolatries, like Jeremiah, the last of the pre-exile prophets, denouncing the cult of the 'Queen of the Heavens'.

No other civilization, therefore, seems to have made the principle of sexual difference so crystal clear: between the two sexes there is a cleavage, an abyss, which is marked by their different relationships to the Law (religious and political) and which is the very condition of their alliance. Monotheistic unity is sustained by a radical separation of the sexes: indeed, this separation is its prerequisite. For without this gap between the sexes, without this localization of the polymorphic, orgasmic body, laughing and desiring, in the other sex, it would have been impossible, in the symbolic sphere, to isolate the principle of One Law — One, Purifying, Transcendent, Guarantor of the ideal interest of the community. In the sphere of reproductive relations (at that time inseparably linked to relations of *production*) it would have been impossible to insure the propagation of the race by making it the only acceptable end of *jouissance*.

There is one unity: an increasingly purified community discipline, isolated as a transcendent principle and thus insuring the survival of the group. This *unity* that the God of monotheism represents is sustained by a desire that pervades the community, making it run but also threatening it. Remove this threatening desire — this perilous support of the community — from man; place it beside him: you have woman, who is speechless, but who appears as the pure desire of speech, or who insures, on the human side, the permanence of the divine paternal function: that is, the desire to propagate the race.

A nation of shepherds, nomads, who settle only temporarily to found their community by means of the only durable bond in steppe and desert: the word. The shepherd (Abel, for example) will be sacrificed, then, so that an ephemeral farmer

19

can initiate the recitation of the tribal wanderings. There follow, in addition, exiles and invasions: a sixth century B.C. of exodus, a fifth century of temporary return to the land, with the invaders displaying a relative degree of tolerance. The word of the community will oscillate, then, between prophecy and legislation; but it will always be a language whose goal is the reassembly of this society that history is bent on dispersing. We must not use some specious sociologizing to attribute to socio-historic or climactic conditions the privilege obtained in the southern Mediterranean basin by the word and the monotheistic transcendence that represents its instance. But the discovery, by one of the peoples of this region, of that specific form of religiosity which is monotheism (and which had failed in Egypt after the attempts of Amen-Hotep IV), corresponds, on the one hand, to the function of human symbolism: to provide an instance of communication and cohesion despite the fact that it operates by dividing (thing/word, body/speech, pleasure/law, incest/procreation). . . . On the other hand, and simultaneously, it represents the paternal function: patrilinear descent with transmission of the father's name centralizes eroticism in the single goal of procreation, in the grip of an abstract symbolic authority which refuses to acknowledge the fact that the child grows and is carried in the mother's body, which a matrilinear system of descent kept alive in the mind by leaving certain possibilities of polymorphism — if not incest — still available. If, with these two keys, one can consolidate a social whole and make it resistant to the tests of internal or external dissolution, one begins to understand that the community which uses it obtains a vitality which allows it not only to survive geographic or historical threats, but to insure an otherwise impossible development of productive forces by means of an infinite perfecting of goods and technology. Productivist teleology is insured by this control: that the threats of the prophets harry this teleology and keep it from degenerating into profiteering and the enjoyment of wealth does not in any sense preclude the advantage that the wealthy classes derive from it for the perfecting of their economic and political power.

The economy of this mechanism requires that women be excluded from the single true and legislating principle, from The Word, as well as from the (always paternal) face which accords to procreation its social value: excluded from knowledge and from power. The myth of the relationship between Eve and the serpent is the best summary of this exclusion: the serpent stands for the inverse of God, since he invites Eve to transgress God's prohibition. But it is also this very desire to transgress which Adam represses, which he dares not act out, which is his shame: the sexual symbolism helps us understand that the serpent is that which, in God or Adam, remains outside or beyond the sublimated content of the Word. Eve has no relationship except with that — precisely because she is its opposite, the 'other race'.

When Yahweh says to the serpent, 'I will put enmity between thee and woman, and between thy seed (*zera*) and her seed (*zera*): it shall bruise thy head, and thou shalt bruise its heel (*akev*)' — He establishes the divergence — of 'race', of 'seed' — between God and man on the one hand and woman on the other. Furthermore, in the second part of the sentence, woman disappears altogether into seed: generation. But, even more essentially, God formulates the code of eroticism between the two sexes as though it were a code of war. A war without end: where *he* will lose his head (or his gland?), *she*, her footprint, her limit, her succession (the threat to deprive her of the act of generation if she takes herself to be all-powerful, phallic). A strange goal, in any case, to follow on the heels of women: let's keep it in mind when we see the bound feet of Chinese women, bruised in a process that is infinitely less drastic, but more painful and (God knows) more certain.

St. Augustine returns to and defines this function of the serpent when he points out that it represents the 'corporeal sense' but belongs to 'the rational nature' and 'is dependent on the intelligence': and when he thinks that (must we believe that this is a consequence of the double nature of the 'corporeal sense'?) the sexual difference, far from being a question of distinction between two individuals, is 'to be found in each human being, considered individually'.

21

Therefore I wanted to see in her [woman] the symbol of a privilege which animals do not have; so I thought it was necessary to see the *serpent* in the *corporeal sense* . . . We are speaking here of a sense which belongs to the rational nature and stems from the intelligence. The corporeal sense is divided into five separate senses, and may be defined as that which permits men and animals to perceive forms and bodily motions . . . When the attention of the soul, which thus exercises its active function on the temporal and corporeal things with that speed characteristic of reason, is attracted by this carnal and animal sense which leads it to *delight in itself* — in other words, when the soul searches for its selfish and particular good to the neglect of the *common general good* which belongs to everyone and which is *immutable*, then, one might say, the serpent speaks to the woman. To consent to this attraction is to eat the forbidden fruit. (*De Trinitate*, italics mine)

If what woman desires is the opposite of the sublimating word and the paternal law, she herself cannot *have* or *be* that opposite. All that remains to her is to pit herself constantly against that opposite in the very gesture by which she desires it, to kill it endlessly and then suffer continuously: a radiant perspective on the masochism at the price of which she may be Queen. In a symbolic productive/reproductive economy centered on the Paternal Word (the Phallus, if you like), one can make a woman believe that she *is* (the Phallus, if you like) even if she doesn't have it (the serpent — the penis): Doesn't she have the child? In this way, social harmony is preserved: the structure functions, produces, and reproduces. Without it, the very foundation of this society is endangered.

We must insist on this last point, which is of unsuspected importance. One betrays, at best, one's naïveté if one considers our modern societies to be simply patrilinear, or 'class-structured', or capitalist-monopolist, and ignores the fact that they are at the same time (and never one without the other) governed by a monotheism whose essence is best expressed in the Bible: the paternal Word sustained by a fight to the finish between the two races (men/women). In this naïveté, one forgets that whatever attacks this radical codification of the sexual difference and still remains within the framework of our patrilinear, class-structured, capitalist societies is attacking — primarily and in the same blow — a fundamental discovery of Judaism that resides in the separation of the sexes and in their incompatibility: in castration, if you like — the support of monotheism and the source of its eroticism. To wish to deny this separation and yet remain within the framework of patrilinear capitalist society and its monotheistic ideology (even disguised as humanism) necessarily plunges one into the petty perversion of fetishism. And we know the role that the pervert — invincibly believing in the maternal phallus, obstinately refusing the existence of the other sex — has been able to play in antisemitism and the totalitarian movements that embrace it. Let us remember the fascist or socialist homosexual community (and all homosexual communities for whom there is no 'other race'), inevitably flanked by a community of Amazons who have forgotten the war of the sexes and identify with the paternal word and its serpent. The feminist movements are equally capable of such perverse denials of the Biblical teaching. We must recognize this and be on our guard.

On the other hand, there are analysts who do recognize this, and, faithful to Freudian pessimism, accept the abyss between the two races; yet they preach the impossibility of communication between the two, the lack of 'rapport'. It is no longer a question here of the war between the sexes: doesn't every psychiatrist have as a companion some 'dead woman', some asphasic mother, some inaudible harbour of procreation, to insure, to reassure, the 'analytic word'?

The solution? To go on waging the war of the sexes without respite, without a perverse denial of the abyss that marks the sexual difference or a disillusioned mortification at its depth, while some other economy of the sexes works itself out; but not before it has revolutionized our entire logic of production (class) and reproduction (family). China will only be another horizon, understandable once this total change is effected, and susceptible, without it, to being cast as another perversion, another mortification (for example: the blindness of the leftist who believes in Chinese chastity — at last the discovery of a happiness that goes against 'bourgeois morality'.)

III

The Virgin of the Word

Universalist as it is, Christianity associates women as well with the symbolic order, but only on the condition that they maintain their virginity. If they don't, they may expiate their carnal pleasure by some form of *martyrdom*. Between these two extremes, a mother participates in the community of the Christian Word not by giving birth to her children, but by preparing them for baptism.

Augustine again offers a rather cynical explanation for the primarily economic reasons for this association of women with the Christian Word at the price of the virginity represented by Mary and imitated by the female monastic orders. Quite simply, since Augustine's time, and in European countries, the survival of the community no longer depends on the accelerated propagation of the race, but rather on the participation by all men and women in symbolic efforts (technical as well as ideological) for the perfection of the means and relationships of production.

> But, in our age, when serving Christ no longer means propagating the race, since he will no longer come to us descended from the flesh, it would be sheer foolishness to burden oneself, for the pleasure of marrying, with these tribulations of the flesh that the Apostle predicts for those who wish to marry; unless, finding oneself unable to remain chaste, one has to fear being tempted by Satan and falling into guilty promiscuity. (*On the Holy Virginity*, XVI, 16)

Between this historical constraint and the myth of the Virgin impregnated by the Word there is a certain distance, which will be bridged by two psychoanalytical methods: one is relative to the role of the mother, the other to the function of language.

The first consists in ceasing to repress the fact that the mother is *other*, has no penis, but experiences *jouissance* and bears children. But this acknowledgment is made only at the preconscious level: just enough to imagine that she bears children, but not that she has participated in an act of coitus, in a 'primitive scene'. Once more, the vagina and the *jouissance* of the mother are disregarded, and immediately replaced by that which puts the mother on the side of the socio-symbolic community: childbearing, procreation in the name of the father. This false recognition — non-recognition — of maternal *jouissance* is accomplished by a process whose source Ernest Jones was the first to understand. Too hastily dismissed as simply the biographer of Freud, Jones deserves credit not only for having proposed one of the most interesting concepts of female sexuality, but for having been the first to attempt an analysis of the sexual economy of the great Christian myths. So, in the Word and Breath celebrated by many religions of which Christianity is the chief, the psychoanalyst sees an emanation not of the glottal sphincter, but of the anal. This sacrilegious theory, confirmed by the fantasies of patients, tends to prove that impregnation by the fart (hiding behind its sublimation into Word) corresponds to the fantasy of anal pregnancy, the fantasy of penetration or self-penetration by an anal penis, and the fantasy of an identification of anus and vagina: i.e. a denial of the sexual difference. Such a scenario is probably more frequent in male subjects, and represents the way in which the little boy usurps the role of the mother, by denying his difference in order to submit himself in her place and as a woman to the father. In this homosexual economy, we see that what Christianity recognizes in a woman, what it demands of her in order to place her within its symbolic order, is this: while living or thinking of herself as a virgin impregnated by the Word, she lives and thinks of herself as a male homosexual. If, on the other hand, this identification with the homosexual does not succeed, if a woman is not virgin, nun, and chaste, but has orgasms and gives birth, her only means of complying with the symbolic paternal order is to engage in an endless battle between her sexual maternal body and the symbolic prohibition — a battle that will take the form of guilt and mortification, and will culminate in masochistic *jouissance*. For a woman who has not easily repressed her relationship with her mother, participation in the symbolic paternal order as Christianity defines it can only be masochistic. As Augustine again so marvellously puts it: 'As far as I think, however, no one would dare prefer virginity to martyrdom.' (*On the Holy Virginity*, XLVII, 47) The ecstatic and the melancholic, two great Christian feminine archetypes, exemplify two ways by which a woman may participate in this symbolic Christian order.

In the case of the ecstatic, the mother is denied and her attributes are displaced onto the symbolic father. The woman then submits herself to a sexually undifferentiated androgynous being:

> Thus, when this Immortal Husband wants with such profusion to enrich a soul with the abundance of his grace, he binds it so tightly to himself that, overwhelmed by happiness, the soul falls into his arms, as though in a swoon. All it can do is be supported by him, and receive this delicious *milk* which nourishes it, fortifies it, sustains it, and makes it fit to be honoured by new favours, which, in turn, prepare it for even greater ones. After the soul has returned from this blessed drunkenness, as from a deep sleep, it finds itself so astonished that it seems that, in this trance, in this *holy madness*, it can utter these words: The milk that flows from your breasts, O my *divine husband*, is sweeter than wine, and its fragrance surpasses the most excellent perfumes. (Theresa d'Avila, *On The Love of God*)

In the case of the melancholic (and often evidence of both types exists in one act or individual), submission to the father is experienced as punishment, pain, and suffering inflicted upon

27

the heterogeneous body. Such a confrontation provokes a melancholy *jouissance* whose most vivid eulogy, perhaps, is found in Catherine of Siena's treatise on the sensual delight of tears.

What is there in the psycho-sexual development of a little girl in monotheistic capitalist society that moulds her to this economy in which her access to the social order (to power, knowledge, symbolism) must be found within these two limits?

There is increasing insistence on the importance of the pre-Oedipal phases (oral and anal) to the subsequent development of both boy and girl. The child is bound to the mother's body without that body being, as yet, 'another'. Rather, the mother's body exists with the child's in a sort of natural/social continuum. This phase is dominated by the oral and anal impulses (incorporation and aggressive rejection): hence the pleasure is auto-erotic as well as inseparable from the body of the mother. With the Oedipal phase come language, the symbolic instance, the ban on auto-eroticism, and the recognition of the function of the father. As Jones, again, points out, the boy as well as the girl must renounce his/her pleasure in order to find an object of the opposite sex, or renounce his/her sex to find a homogeneous pleasure without 'another' as its object. But if such is the rule, it is realized differently in boys and in girls.

When the boy does not identify with his mother to submit like a woman to his father, he becomes his father's rival for the love of his mother. The castration that he experiences in this situation is rather a fear of 'aphanisis': fear of not being ably to satisfy both her and himself. The girl finds herself faced with a choice as well: either she identifies with her mother, or she raises herself to the symbolic stature of her father. In the first case, the pre-Oedipal phases (oral and anal eroticism) are intensified. By giving herself a male object (substitute for the father), she desires and appropriates him for herself through that which her mother has willed her during the 'feminine' pre-Oedipal phase — i.e. across the oral-sadistic veil that accompanies the vaginal *jouissance* of heterosexual woman. If we perceive a sort of fundamental female homosexuality in this pre-Oedipal identification with the mother, we perceive at the same time that this has nothing whatever to do with male homosexuality, and is not transcended by 'the female heterosexual'. In the second case, identification with the father, the daughter represses the oral-sadistic phase, and at the same time represses the vagina and the possibility of finding an 'opposite' partner. (This situation can be achieved by refusal of the male partner, feminization of the male partner, or by assuming either a male or a female role in a relationship with a female partner.) The sadistic component of such an economy is so violent as to totally obliterate the vagina. In her fantasy, the girl obtains a real or imaginary penis for herself; and the fantasy penis seems here to be less important than the access she gains to the symbolic dominance which is necessary to censor the pre-Oedipal phase and wipe out the last traces of dependence on the body of the mother. Obliteration of the pre-Oedipal phase, identification with the father, and then: 'I am looking, as a man would, for a woman'; or else, 'I submit myself, as if I were a man who thought he was a woman, to a woman who thinks she is a man.' Such are the double or triple twists of what we commonly call female homosexuality. The oral-sadistic dependence on the mother has been so strong that it now represents not simply a veil over the vagina, but a veritable blockade. Thus the lesbian never discovers the vagina, but makes of this restitution of pre-Oedipal impulses (oral/anal; absorption/rejection) a powerful symbolic mechanism. Artist or intellectual, she wages a vigilant war against her pre-Oedipal dependence on her mother, which keeps her from discovering her own body as other, different, possessing a vagina. A melancholy — fear of aphanisis — punctuated by sudden thrills marks the loss of this maternal body, this urgent investment of the symbolic with the sadistic.

It is interesting to note that in the development of speech, the pre-Oedipal phase corresponds to an intense echolalia, first in rhythm and then in intonation, before the phonologico-syntactic structure is imposed on the sentence. This latter is not considered to be perfectly achieved until the end of the Oedipal phase. It is evident, therefore, that a re-activation of the pre-Oedipal phase in a man (by homosexuality or by imaginary incest) recreates in his speech this pre-sentence-making dis-

29

position to rhythm, intonation, nonsense; makes nonsense
abound within sense: makes him laugh. When he flees the
symbolic paternal order (by fear of castration, Freud would
say; Jones would say fear of asphanisis), man can laugh. But,
on the contrary, the daughter is handed the keys to the symbolic order when she identifies with the father: only there is
she recognized not in herself but against her rival, the vaginal,
jouissante mother. Thus, at the price of censuring herself as a
woman, she will be able to bring to triumph her henceforth
sublimated sadistic attacks on the mother whom she has
repressed and with whom she will never cease to fight, either
(as a heterosexual) by identifying with her, or (as a homosexual) by pursuing her as erotic object. Therefore the rush of
these nonsensical, periphrastic, maternal rhythms in her speech,
far from soothing her, far from making her laugh, destroys
her symbolic armour: makes her ecstatic, nostalgic, or mad.
Nietzsche would not have known how to be a woman. A
woman has nothing to laugh about when the paternal order
falls. She can take pleasure in it if, by identifying with the
mother, the vaginal body, she imagines herself to be the
repressed and sublimated content of the culture rising through
its cracks. If, on the other hand, she has failed to identify with
the mother, and — as victim or militant — found her one
superficial, backward, and easily severed hold on life in the
symbolic paternal order, its dissolution can be her death.

Faithful to a certain vein of Biblical tradition, Freud found
the fear of castration central to all psychology, male or female.
Closer to Christianity, but also to the post-Romantic psychology which defines all natures according to their relation to
love, Jones proposed to find the determining factor in psychic
structure rather in aphanisis (the fear of losing the possibility
of gratification), than in castration. I do not think we would
simply be reviving Greek or logico-phenomenological thought
if we were to situate this fundamental factor neither in castration nor in aphanisis (both of which would be only its fanta-
sized derivatives), but rather in *the process of learning the
symbolic function* to which the human animal is subjected
from the pre-Oedipal phase onward. By 'symbolic function'
we mean a system of signs (first, rhythmic and intonational

differences, then signified/signifier) organized into logico-syntactic structures whose goal is to accredit social communication as exchange purified of pleasure. We are speaking, then, of a training process, an inhibition, which begins with the first echolalias, but fully imposes itself with the learning of language. If the pre-Oedipal phase of this inhibition is still full of pleasure and not yet detached from the mother/child continuum, even so, it is fraught with its own prohibitions: notably the training of the glottal and anal sphincters. And it is on the foundation of these prohibitions that the superego is built.

The symbolic order functions in our monotheistic West by means of a system of kinship dependent on transmission of the father's name and a rigorous prohibition of incest, and a system of verbal communication that is increasingly logical, simple, positive, and stripped of stylistic, rhythmic, 'poetic' ambiguities. Such an order brings this *constitutional inhibition of the speaking animal* to a zenith never before attained, which is assumed by the role of the father. The mother's share (the 'repressed') in such an order includes not only the impulses (of which the most basic is the impulse of aggressive rejection) but the earliest training of those impulses (the education of the sphincters) in the oral/anal phases, which is marked by rhythms, intonations, and gestures which as yet have no significance.

Daughter of the father? Or of the mother?

As the Sophoclean chorus says, 'Never was a daughter more her father's child' than Electra. It is she who incites Orestes to vengeance; it is she as well who is the principal agent in the murder of her mother — more so than Orestes himself. Isn't it the voices of the mother and the daughter we hear in the murder scene, while the son remains silent? We can delude ourselves into thinking that Orestes, an anti-Oedipus, has killed his mother to wrest himself thus from the family and move into a new community, supra-familial, political: the *city* whose cult was already becoming an economic and political necessity in Greece. Faced with this murder, planned and spoken by Electra, of which Orestes is only the instrument, one wonders if anti-Oedipal man is not a fiction, or, in any case, if he is not always appended to the *jouissance* of a wife/sister. There

31

would be no unavenged dead father — no resurrection of the father — if that father did not have a (virgin) daughter. A daughter does not put up with the murder of her father. That the father is made a symbolic power — that is, that he is dead, and thus elevated to the rank of a Name — is what gives meaning to her life, which will be an eternal vendetta. Not that this fixation does not drive her mad: in vain Electra says 'Only a madwoman could forget a father killed so pitilessly'; in vain she accuses Chrysothemis, 'her mother's daughter', of being demented, of forgetting her father: she, Electra, cannot keep herself from being driven mad by her own activity. But her madness, contrary to Chrysothemis' passive clinging to the mother, is what the chorus will call, at the end of the play, an 'effort that crowns history'. Without it, there would be no freedom, no history for the city from which, as woman, she is alienated nonetheless. For, in fact, this pursuit of the cause of the father is the product of a much darker motivation: hatred of the mother, or, more precisely, hatred of the mother's *jouissance*. Electra wants Clytemnestra's death not because Clytemnestra is a mother who kills the father, but because she is (Aegisthus') mistress. That *jouissance* be forbidden to the mother: this is the demand of the father's daughter, fascinated by her mother's *jouissance*. And one can imagine how much the city will depend on these fathers' daughters (given that a man can play the role of 'daughter') to make its citizens forget that the *jouissance* of the mother is nourished by the war between the sexes and ends in the murder of the father. The Electras — deprived forever of their hymen — militants in the cause of their fathers, frigid with exaltation — are dramatic figures where the social consensus corners any woman who wants to escape her condition: nuns, 'revolutionaries', 'feminists'.

It takes a Mozart to make a comedy out of this loyalty of daughter to father. Keep the dead father: the Commander. Cut out Orestes and replace him with poor Ottavio. Aegisthus and Clytemnestra have no reason to exist: Don Giovanni himself will represent power and pleasure following one upon the other in a radiant, musical infinity. So the heroic Electra becomes the pitiful, unhappy Donna Anna: the ill-treated hysteric, passionately in love with her father's death, commemorating his murder — but without hope of revenge — in a hallucinatory monologue of bitterness and jubilation. Since history repeats itself only as farce, Donna Anna is a farcical Electra: still a slave to her father, but to a father whose law and politics are crumbling enough, by the eighteenth century, to allow Mozart to avoid making such a tragedy of it.

IV

Outside Time

The symbolic order — the order of verbal communication, the paternal order of descent — is a temporal order. For the speaking animal, it is the clock of objective time: it provides the reference point, and, consequently, all possibilities of measurement, by defining a past, a present, and a future. If *I* don't exist except in the language I address to another, I am only *present* in the moment of that communication. In relation to this present of my being, there is that which precedes and that which follows. My family lineage as well will be placed in this before and after: the ranks of ancestors and future generations. And between such co-ordinates I will project myself: a journey on the axis which stands for my own genealogy and is centered on the moment of my speech, its most intimate phenomenon. This projection will not be a mere displacement of my *present* to some point further on, or onto somebody else: the projection itself may overthrow the well-oiled order of communication (and, thus, society) or of descent (and thus of the family), if I project not my fixed, governed word, ruled by the common series of taboos and inhibitions (sexual, grammatical, political, economic, ideological), but rather the underlying causality that shapes it, which I repress in order that I may enter the socio-symbolic order, and which is capable of blowing the whole thing apart.

'Underlying causality' — a figure of speech that alludes to the social contradictions that a given society can provisionally gag in order to constitute itself as such. But a figure of speech

34

used to designate that other terrain as well: unconscious, impulsive, trans-verbal, whose eruptions determine not only my speech or my inter-personal relationships, but the complex relations of production and reproduction which we so frequently mistake as dependent on, rather than shaping, the economy.

No reference point in the unconscious; I haven't come to that yet. No present, no past, no future. No true or false either. It displaces, condenses, distributes. It retains all that's repressed by the Word: by sign, by sense, by communication, by symbolic order, in whatever is legislating, restrictive, paternal.

There is no time without speech. Therefore, no time without the father. That's what the father means: sign and time. It is understandable, then, that what the father doesn't say about the unconscious, what sign and time repress in the impulses, appears as their *truth* (if there is no absolute, what is truth, if not the unspoken of the spoken?) and that this truth can be imagined only as a woman.

A curious truth: outside time, with neither past nor future, neither true nor false; buried underground, it neither postulates nor judges. It refuses, displaces, breaks the symbolic order before it can re-establish itself.

If a woman cannot be part of the temporal symbolic order except by identifying with the father, it is clear that as soon as she shows any evidence of that which, in herself, escapes such identification and acts differently, resembling the dream or the maternal body, she evolves into this 'truth' in question. It is thus that feminine specificity defines itself in patrilineal society: woman is a specialist in the unconscious, a witch, a bacchanalian, taking her *jouissance* in an anti-Apollonian, Dionysian orgy.

A *jouissance* which breaks the symbolic chain, the dominance, the taboo. A *marginal speech*, with regard to the science, religion, and philosophy of the *polis* (witch, child, underdeveloped, not even a poet, at best a poet's accomplice). A *pregnancy*: escape from the bonds of daily social temporality, interruption of the regular monthly cycles: woman deserts the surfaces — skin, eyes — so that she may descend to the depths of the body, to hear, taste, smell the infinitesimal life

35

of the cells. Perhaps it is only another myth that the period of gestation approaches a 'cosmic' and 'objective' sense of time as opposed to the ordinary 'human', 'subjective' one: a myth designed to validate time (even though its 'nature' is different) at the very moment when time is dissolving, before its product (the child) results. The child: sole evidence, for the symbolic order, of *jouissance* and pregnancy; the child, thanks to whom the woman, herself an instrument localized in time, will be coded into the chain of generations. *Jouissance*, pregnancy, marginal speech: the means by which this 'truth', cloaked and hidden by the symbolic order and its companion, time, functions through women.

The artist (that make believe Oedipus) suspects that his unverified atemporal truth springs from the side of the mother. The western artist (that fetishist), then, exalts this truth by finding its symbol in the female body. Let's not even speak about the endless 'Madonnas with Child'. Let's take something less evangelical: Tiepolo's *Time Disrobing Truth* (Boston Museum of Fine Arts) for example. A rape scene, or a scene of coitus? The enigma is emphasized by the anomaly of the design. Truth has a right leg where her left should be, and this leg is thrust forward, between herself and the genitals of Time. But perhaps his pain and her air of majesty are not really deceptive: their gaze into each other's eyes is caught by two others who do not speak: the infant and the parakeet. The arrows (of love?) and a mask are there to indicate the indirect methods by which 'Truth', so armed, can not only trample the earth, but steal its 'false' from Time and transform Time into a fallen lord, an angry servant. But in this fantasy where a woman, intended to represent Truth, takes the place of the phallus (notably in Tiepolo's painting), she ceases to act as atemporal, unconscious, splitting, destroying, and breaking the temporal and symbolic order; rather, she substitutes herself for it as solar mistress, priestess of the absolute. When Truth is stripped in order to be presented as itself, 'truth' is lost within itself; for in fact it has no self, it only rises between the cracks of an identity. But once it is given form — as a woman, for example — the 'truth' of the unconscious passes into the symbolic order, it even over-shadows it, as funda-

36

mental fetish, phallus-substitute, support for all transcendental divinity. A crude but enormously effective trap for feminism: to acknowledge us, to make us into the truth of the temporal order, so as to keep us from functioning as its unconscious 'truth', formless beyond true, and false, beyond present-past-future.

It seems to me that, far from being simply a matter of 'others' stubbornly refusing the specificity of women, this double bind, which has always succeeded in the West, arises from a profound structural mechanism concerning the casting of sexual differences and even of speech in the West. A woman is caught there, and can't do too much about it. Let me note a few concrete results of this implacable structure:

We cannot gain access to the temporal scene, i.e. to political affairs, except by identifying with the values considered to be masculine (dominance, superego, the endorsed communicative word that institutes stable social exchange). From Louise Michel to A. Kollantaï, to cite only two relatively recent examples, not to speak of the suffragettes or their contemporary Anglo-Saxon sisters, some of whom are more threatening than the fathers of the primitive horde — we have been able to serve or overthrow the socio-historic order by playing supermen. A few enjoy it: the most active, the most effective, the gays (whether or not they're aware of it). Others, more bound to their mothers, more tuned in as well to their unconscious impulses, refuse this role and hold themselves back, sullen, neither speaking nor writing, in a permanent state of expectation punctuated now and then by some kind of outburst: a cry, a refusal, an 'hysterical symptom'. These two extremes condemn us either to being the most passionate bureaucrats of the temporal order (the new wave: women ministers), or to engaging in subversive activity (the other new wave, always following a bit behind the first: promotion of women in the left). Or else we remain in an eternal sulk before history, politics, society: the symptoms of their failure, but symptoms betrothed to marginality or to a new mysticism.

To refuse both these extremes. To know that an ostensibly masculine, paternal (because supportive of time and symbol) identification is necessary in order to have some voice in the record of politics and history. To achieve this identification in order to escape a smug polymorphism where it is so easy and comfortable for a woman here to remain; and by this identification to gain entry to social experience. To be wary from the first of the premium on narcissism that such an integration may carry with it: to reject the validity of homologous woman, finally virile; and to act, on the socio-politico-historical stage, as her negative: that is, to act first with all those who 'swim against the tide', all those who refuse — all the rebels against the existing relations of production and reproduction. But neither to take the role of revolutionary (male or female): to refuse all roles, in order, on the contrary, to summon this timeless 'truth' — formless, neither true nor false, echo of our *jouissance*, of our madness, of our pregnancies — into the order of speech and social symbolism. But how? By listening; by recognizing the unspoken in speech, even revolutionary speech; by calling attention at all times to whatever remains unsatisfied, repressed, new, eccentric, incomprehensible, disturbing to the *status quo*.

A constant alternation between time and its 'truth', identity and its loss, history and the timeless, signless, extra-phenomenal things that produce it. An impossible dialectic: a permanent alternation: never the one without the other. It is not certain that anyone here and now is capable of it. An analyst conscious of history and politics? A politician tuned into the unconscious? A woman perhaps. . . .

V

I Who Want Not To Be

For a woman, the call of the mother is not only a call beyond time, beyond the socio-political battle. With family and history at an impasse, this call troubles the Word. It generates voices, 'madness', hallucinations. After the superego, the ego, that fragile envelope, founders and sinks. It is helpless to stave off the eruption of this conflict, of this love which has bound the little girl to her mother and then lain in wait for her — black lava — all along the path of her desperate attempt to identify with the symbolic paternal order. Once the moorings of the ego begin to slip, life itself can't hang on: slowly, gently, death settles in. Suicide without a cause, or silent sacrifice for an apparent cause which, in our age, is usually political: a woman can carry off such things without tragedy, without even drama. She can carry them off as though it were simply a matter of making an inevitable, irresistible, self-motivated transition, rather than fleeing a well-fortified front.

I think of Virginia Woolf, who sank wordlessly into the river, her pockets weighted with stones. Haunted by voices, by waves, by lights, in love with colours — blue, green — seized by a sort of bizarre gaiety that brought on the fits of strangled, hooting, uncontrollable laughter remembered by Miss Brown.

Or I think of the dark corner of the deserted farmhouse in the Russian countryside where, a few months later in that same year, 1941, Maria Tsvetaieva hanged herself, fleeing the war. Tsvetaieva, the most rhythmic of Russian poets, whose drumbeats went further back in the memory of the Russian language than even Mayakovsky's, and who wrote:

> My problem (in writing poetry, and my reader's problem
> in understanding my poems) consists in the impossibility
> of my task: for example, to express the sigh a-a-a- with
> words (that is, meanings). With words/meanings to say
> the sound. So that all that remains for the ear is a-a-a-.

Or Sylvia Plath, yet another woman disillusioned with words
and meanings, fled to the refuge of lights, rhythms, sounds: a
refuge that already announces, for those who know how to
read, the silence with which she will abandon life*:

> Axes
> After whose stroke the wood rings
> And the echoes!
> Echoes travelling
> Off from the centre like horses.
>
>
> Words dry and riderless,
> The indefatigable hoof-taps.
> While
> From the bottom of the pool, fixed stars
> Govern a life.

When Dostoyevsky's Kirilov commits suicide, it's to prove
that his will is stronger than God's. By proving thus that the
human *I* possesses supreme power, he believes he is emancipat-
ing man by putting him in the place of God. ('If I kill myself
I become God' — 'God is a necessity and therefore He must
exist.')

Something entirely different is at stake in Tsvetaieva's
suicide: not *to be*, that is, in the final instance, *to be God*; but
to dissolve being itself, to free it of the Word, of God, of self.
'I don't want to die. I want not to be,' she says in her notes.

In an analogous situation a man can imagine an all-powerful
though always insignificant mother, to 'legitimize' himself:
to make himself known, to lean on her and be guided by her

---

*From *Ariel* p.86 (Faber).

through the social labyrinth, though not without his own running ironic commentary. Méry-Laurent for Mallarmé, Madame Straus for 'little Marcel', Miss Weaver for Joyce, the series of fiancées taken and rejected by Kafka. . . . For a woman, as soon as the father's not calling the dance and language is being torn apart by rhythm, no mother can serve as an axis for the sacred or the farce. The girl tries herself: the result is so-called female homosexuality, identification with men, or a tight rein on the least pre-Oedipal pleasure. And if no paternal 'legitimization' comes along to dam up the inexhaustible non-symbolized impulse, she collapses into psychosis or suicide.

The triumph of narcissism? But that would be the most primal form of narcissism: the most archaic death wish, that which precedes and, thus, that which surpasses all identity, all sign, all order, and all belief. As a motive of revolutionary action, this impulse, strangled in the throat of history, can destroy the body itself. For Tsvetaieva, the failure of the Revolution, soviet bureaucracy, the war, are all to be considered, all the ostensible reasons. But without faith — without testament.

So, through identifying with the father, she strives for access to the Word and to time, and thus becomes a support of transcendence. But isn't a woman also the most radical atheist, the most committed anarchist, when she is carried away by what the symbolic order rejects? In the eyes of this society, such a posture casts her as a victim. But elsewhere?

These themes, these names: were they chosen by chance, according to mood or desire? Of course; and my own subjectivity is only too obvious. But they are also, perhaps, names and themes that betray us here for what two thousand years of history have made us, and as we remain, intact, beside or beyond all movements or battles, social revolutions or access to the pill. Could those be the lenses that keep us from seeing China? The same lenses which, if adjusted, might bring it into our field of vision? But understanding China will involve much more than fitting these lenses over the reality of China as it is given to us by sinology, by contemporary history, or by our own observations. To do so during our journey through China would mean that the reality of China is accessible through our models, our habits; that it lends itself to our way of seeing. I'm not saying that this reality is invisible to the Westerner, who is condemned forever to the relativity of his knowledge. I'm saying only that we must adjust our glasses before trying to look close up at what's going on on the other side. In the meantime, the notes that follow are nothing but a first hesitant step in that direction.

CHINESE WOMEN

I

The Mother at the Centre

The present revolution in the Chinese family, and, hence, in the status of women in China, is part of an effort that has been going on since the beginning of this century. It is a difficult revolution to outline, particularly because the history of Chinese society provides us with two different conceptions of the family.

The first model is hypothetical (utopian? imaginary?) and is drawn essentially from peasant customs represented in folklore and substantiated by some of the writings of Marcel Granet (*La Civilisation Chinoise*, La Renaissance du Livre, 1929). It approaches Engels' famous 'matriarchy', discussed and refuted so many times by modern anthropologists. From other studies by Marcel Granet (*Catégories matrimoniales et relations de proximités dans la Chine ancienne*, 1939) discussed and interpreted by Claude Lévi-Strauss (*Les Structures Elémentaires de la parenté*, Mouton, 1947 (1967)), it would seem that this 'matrilinear family', 'primitive commune', or 'matriarchy' conforms to the well-known anthropological category termed 'restricted exchange with bilateral descent' (meaning that each individual has two points of reference, maternal and paternal).

The second model is already an 'agnatic family' with 'unilateral patrilineal descent'. In its primitive form, it retains some traces of the first model, and is the simple generalized exchange in which marriage is practised exclusively with the daughter of the maternal uncle. The model evolves into the general patrilinear exchange which characterizes the patriarchal Confucian family that the socialist revolution is still fighting against. But even among the nobility who conformed to the

Confucian rite, vestiges of the earlier model are highly evident. What about the survival of the matrilinear tradition in the countryside? What about the attitudes of women themselves toward the differences in matrimonial order in the two families? As one would suspect, there is very little information on these subjects to be found in documents written by literate Confucians. One thing is certain: a revolution in the rules of kinship took place in China, and can be traced to sometime around 1000 B.C. A similar occurrence may be detected at about that time in the neighbouring regions of the Mediterranean; but in China it is particularly marked by the fact that the new patriarchal model preserved a greater number of elements from the earlier model. This was doubtless due on the one hand to the extraordinarily advanced development which the matrilinear family had achieved in a highly civilized society with stable institutions; and, on the other hand, to the fact that the feudal order which followed, in order to remain an essentially warring and symbolic culture, was more agrarian than pastoral, more sedentary than nomadic, and depended profitably on the forms of the previous system, though substituting different contents.

What is this 'matrilinear descent' of ancient China?

It consists of a restricted exchange between two exogamous groups ('the men's dynasty' and 'the woman's dynasty') with *matrilinear descent* (dominant in all known restricted exchanges). In addition, it is *matrilocal*: a rather extraordinary custom, since it puts males at a disadvantage (to avoid this disadvantage, matrilinear societies are generally patrilocal, so that even if the children are considered to descend from the maternal line, the father has the 'political power': a lovely situation which some see as the social embodiment of the biological asymmetry of the sexes). A certain preponderance of woman could, however, have been logically necessary in archaic times, and would explain a *matrilinear* and *matrilocal* descent not only by the importance of reproduction for the survival of the race, but by the fact of the premature birth of the 'young of man', a specifically human phenomenon which renders all comparison with animal society or primitive human society null and void. In fact, might not the dominance of the

mother be the first sign of education, civilization? The matrilinear, matrilocal situation is considered dramatic, however,
by the modern anthropologist; if he doesn't make it a source
of some para-psychoanalytic or para-fictional essay, he regards
it as a dark age in which men had not yet resolved the paradox
in their role as 'takers of wives and givers of sisters', as
'authors and victims of their own exchanges'. Such a conception sets aside the study of this kind of maternally dominated
restricted exchange (matrilinear and matrilocal) — a study
more difficult for analytical reasons than for want of examples
— as something other than a simple inversion of a paternally
dominated (patrilinear and patrilocal, or bilinear with paternal
power) restricted exchange. Some of Granet's works, to the
contrary, attempt to describe this restricted exchange between
two exogamous, matrilinear, and matrilocal groups, without,
however, pointing out the social, logical and psychological
consequences such a system had on those outside it (derived
from or appended to it).

Marcel Granet[1] draws his conclusions essentially from folk
dance and legend, but also by deduction from documents
concerning the patrilinear family. The division of the sexes
would coincide, in peasant custom, with the division of labour;
so that the group of men would be opposed to the group of
women as two 'corporations' of workers — field labourers and
weavers. Different in terms of the mode and place of their
work, but complementary in terms of the survival of the community: the entire social organization in China, up through
the most refined ideological systems, seems to be deeply
imprinted with this division into groups that are sexual and
economic at once. Thus, the basic constitutional prohibition of
all society (isolating two groups between which exchanges,
marriage, alliances are contracted) comes between the two
sexes and simultaneously between two categories of workers;
but also between two *territories*. Not only does each group
(sexo-economic) have its own zone within a single village; a

---

[1]Cf. *La Civilisation Chinoise, 1929*, and, with another orientation,
in *Catégories matrimoniales et relations de proximité dans la Chine
ancienne*, 1939.

male or female individual must choose a marriage partner from another village. Membership in a particular sexo-economic-territorial group is indicated by one's name. We see, then, that the relationship that links people of the same name is not only — and not essentially — a blood or 'family tie' (individual mother/child or father/child kinship, etc.); rather, it includes a whole set of economic, territorial, and sexual relationships. Thus, 'mother' is not the woman who gave birth to you, but rather the most 'respected woman in the community'; 'father' is the husband of the woman who gave birth to you, but also all your paternal uncles, etc. Probably because of the importance at that time of procreation for the survival of the community, but also because the community was sedentary and thus accorded a great deal of importance to their habitat — cooking, clothing, domestic chores — women played a predominant role in the life of the society. The setup provided not only that a woman dominate the organization of the home, and that a man choose his wife from his mother's group, i.e. from among the daughters of his mother's brothers or his father's sisters; it seems to have determined as well that boys be considered objects of exogamous exchange — that, rather than *choose*, they were *chosen*. This maternal, matrilinear, and matrilocal descent seems to have been accompanied by transmission of the name of the mother, identified with the name of the place. In any case, that's what we deduce from the fact that in the second type of family, the patrilinear, the name is a double name (local maternal name and family paternal name).

Two things to remember about this bilateral matrilinear organization:

The first is that the separation of sexo-economic-territorial groups is considered to be radical: rivalry and even war are the rule between them. One is not related to the 'others': there is no familiarity; no feeling, no intimacy flows between the two boundaries. The union, the domestic contract, is only a peace treaty between two adversaries, a sort of code that guarantees commerce and civility, and is, ultimately, just an acknowledgment of the relations of the objective forces between two enemies, who live in a constant state of potential separation and war. The social unity is not an absolute unity that would deny the contradiction which underlines it; and furthermore, within this contradiction, a certain dominance is held by the feminine, maternal side. Even within communities of workers who isolated themselves during the winter into male societies and performed rites that were exclusively male, the participants divided themselves into two groups, one representing the male (*yang*) element, (sun, heat, summer), the other, the female (*yin*) (moon, cold, winter). There, it was difference in age which replaced the sexo-economic-territorial oppositions: the adults played the men, and the young boys, the women.

The second characteristic, which has marked Chinese symbolism since this era, consists in the adherence of the society to the earth, the arable soil; and in the feminine connotation of this soil. The soil is the fertile earth, and the earth where the mother gives birth. Vital, living, life-giving, mother and earth are identical for this society that lives on grain, is bound to the soil, and dependent on the seasonal cycles of plants, animals, human beings, climate. But the soil, by metonymy, also connotes coupling: games, engagements, the marriage of the young. The *place* becomes 'holy' because it is identified with the mother; and, at the same time, with the genitality of rival groups. In China, there are no initiation mysteries: they are replaced by the hierogamic celebration which gives the place its meaning. By celebrating a holy place, one thus celebrates a mothering earth; perhaps not even an all-powerful mother, but the very principle of *genitality*: this alternation of war and union between the sexes. No Father, no unifying Word. A *Mother*: the Ancestress and a *place* of sexual jousting represent the logic and the cohesion of the society. Reading about the dances and the legends of ancient China,[1] one can't help but be struck by an imagination totally oriented toward the genital act. It is not sublimated into a law-giving element that threatens but also consoles and protects. Nor does it absorb an eroticism that would be otherwise repressed. There is no display of desirable fetishes, no transgressive pre-

---

[1] Cf. Marcel Granet, *Danses et Légendes de la Chine ancienne*, V. I and II, P U F, 1959.

occupation with sex; and no sinful and fascinating erogenous zone. The leaps of boys and girls mimicking swallows, moons, water, without really knowing what creature or event they represent, seem tame, even childish in their modesty and simplicity. This, because the *prohibition* (sexual guarantor of the society) has been spoken, and is fully functioning and because this matrilinear family model has nothing to do with what we today call 'sexual freedom'. But this prohibition, rather than withdrawing into itself to produce God, transcendence, religion, inserts itself into and between the bodies of the people. It requires them to separate before identifying with each other, by differentiating themselves infinitely within themselves; and requires that they create their sociality only by confrontation with a radical *other*: another sex, another economy, another territory. The genital act becomes, then, the perfect embodiment not only of the alteration (opposition/ identification) of two bodies, but also of two economies, two places, or two symbolic systems. To make genitality the basis of social organization is to keep it from giving the advantage to either of the terms of the contradiction: one of the bodies, one of the crafts, one of the places, one of the symbols. The 'holy place' with maternal attributes is the emblem of this tendency. Later, the function of the holy place was assumed by dragons. But let's not be too eager to point out their phallic symbolism: we must realize first that the dragon appears only during a time of crisis for the first dynasty whose emblem it becomes; and this appearance, according to Granet, follows a sacrifice. The institution of a transcendental sense of community in whose name one makes sacrifice already tends to abandon 'genital' logic. But this abandonment is slow and incomplete: the dragons are paired and represent the two sexual partners; and even when the dragon evokes the Ancestor, it is the Maternal Ancestor. Phallic mother? Or an attempt to summon the *other*, the feminine and maternal force, before a pure, symbolic, unique and unifying nominal and paternal instance has the chance to crystallize, suspending the contradiction of the two?

Several myths, relative, perhaps, to a later period, preserve traces of the 'maternal age': (matrilinear, bilateral descent,

50

matrilocal family, maternal name). Let me give two examples:
The world is made habitable by Yu the Great (?2198 B.C.) who organizes the lands and the waters by causing the Yellow River to flow when he opens Longmen Pass (The Dragon's Gate); but first he turns his wife to stone. One may say that patrilineal descent is really instituted by this legendary dancer, since from his time onward the Chinese monarchy becomes a hereditary dynasty, passed down from father to son. But for the sake of the dynasty — and beginning with Yu — there are no more mixed collective dances: Yu's creation dance is essentially a masculine dance for a masculine community. Yu dances, however, by leaping on one leg and dragging the other, as did the girls in the peasant festivals. Thus, in some way, he appropriates the feminine function for himself, and transforms it into a symbolic political authority. The myth itself is not fooled by this theft: before becoming creator of the universe, Yu kills his wife, who has caught him dancing. The sacrifice of the other (sex, economy, territory) confers power (symbolic, political) on the self.

Another myth preserves traces of the previous family structure even better: the Queen Goddess Nügua, though not present at the birth of the universe, prevents it from caving in; and, in collaboration with her brother-husband, the legendary King Fuxi, creates man and writing at the same time. One can see Nügua and Fuxi both represented in the stone carvings or engravings of the first century B.C.: human heads, serpents' bodies, dragons' tails, all intertwined. A second century text says this about Nügua:

> According to popular legend, when heaven and earth were formed, there was as yet no human race. Nügua began to fashion men out of yellow earth. But she found the task too great for her strength; so she went and gathered some mud, which she found easier to use. And that's how the nobles were men made of yellow earth, and the poor, who live base and servile lives, were drawn from the mud.

Veneration for the mother is found throughout Chinese history (though no longer in Chinese legend) in the ideology of Taoism, which opposed itself to Confucianism and fostered not only many protests against the social order, but several peasant uprisings as well. 'I alone am nourished by the mother,' says the Tao-te-Ching. Xi Wangmu, the Queen-Mother of the West, who had presided over the dead from her home on Mount Kunlun, becomes, for the Taoists, Mother of the Immortals. In the second century B.C., when a drought aggravated the political and economic crisis of the vast Han empire, the discontent of the peasants was added to palace intrigues: the peasant revolt known as the 'Yellow Turbans' (184 B.C.) led to the fall of the second Han Dynasty, after which that of the 'Red Eyebrows' (A.D. 3) put an end to Wang Mang's efforts to reinstate the first Han. It is interesting to note that, in order to ward off political and economic problems, the emperor did not institute agricultural reforms (as did Qin Shi Huangdi, who is celebrated today in China), but rather clung to the teachings of Confucian moralists: whereas the Yellow Turbans and the Red Eyebrows, clamouring for reforms, claimed descent from Xi Wangmu, the Taoist Queen-Mother of the West. According to the historian Sima Qian, though the first Han emperors worshipped a single divinity, making sacrifice only to Heaven, in 113 the Emperor Wu founded the cult of the Earth — a feminine essence complementary to the Sky. One sacrificed to her at the foot of the mountain rather than at its summit, where the Sky God was worshipped: and rather than burning the offering, one buried it.

Chinese Buddhism, in its turn, adds to the Buddhist pantheon the Goddess Guan Yin, whose cult equals and — for certain sects — surpasses that of the Buddha himself. With Nügua and Xi Wangmu, Guan Yin represents that endurance of the cult of the mother throughout Chinese history, despite and including Confucian ritualism.

We could find other historical and legendary facts to attest to the survival of the prehistoric age and the matrilinear model (bilateral restricted exchange) of the family. But even more important are the repercussions such a social structure had on the ideological conceptions and symbolic customs that have constituted the Chinese nation until modern times. Let us examine two: the conception of causality or 'the divinity': and the functioning of the system of communication (language, writing).

52

From their earliest contacts — through Jesuit missions — with Chinese civilization, European philosophers and theologians have attempted to equate or contrast the western concepts of God, spirit, soul, with the reflections of the Chinese on the workings of the cosmic and social order. Among the numerous works on this subject, I will cite one in particular which, because of the personalities involved and the specific problem they raise, has continued to preoccupy western sinology and philosophy in more secular form. I'm speaking of the *Treatise on Some Aspects of Chinese Religion*, by R. P. Nicolas Longobardi, former Head of the Missionaries of the Society of Jesus in China, printed in Paris in the year 1701, to which are appended some remarks by M. G. G. Leibniz. It is striking to discover the difficulty that both thinkers experienced in confronting the Chinese systems, and the ways in which they deformed those systems in order to assimilate them into their own. For Longobardi, the Chinese does not know 'Our God', because what he represents as a Celestial Emperor, Shang-di, is only an attribute, a quality, of a phenomenal manifestation of the *Li*: matter invested with an immanent mode of 'operation', 'order', 'law', 'action', 'government' — i.e. causality. This causality immanent in matter is disturbing to Father Longobardi: he sees in it — with good reason — the germ of atheism, and discerns quite clearly that the 'divinities' and other 'spirits' who derive from such matter are intended only for the masses, to insure social order and tranquility: they have nothing whatever to do with scholarly thought. In fact, these 'divinities' are simply 'gods of wood and stone, who have only the husk of the Divine'. Another thing that strikes the Reverend Father in this causality immanent in matter which is the *Li*, is that it functions by assuming a radical dichotomy between two terms: (full/empty, life/death, heaven/earth, etc.). The *Li* assures a union or harmony between these poles; but despite and because of this assurance they remain diametrically opposed. For Longobardi, this is reason enough to distrust Chinese doctrine and to refuse to assimilate it into the Christian system, which the Chinese, in any case, are loathe to accept. Leibniz, however, seems interested in the 'immanent causality' of the Chinese system, and his laconic

53

commentary suggests that he is striving to assimilate it into his own effort to evolve the Christian theological conception of causality toward rationalism. In the *Li* he finds 'reason', 'a subtle substance accompanied by perception', 'Descartes would say similar things', etc. He is struck as well by the concreteness of Chinese thought, oriented toward a living, social order. 'They say truth in creatures', 'for perhaps *life, knowledge, authority,* in Chinese are understood *anthropopatos*'. If he approaches, thus, a quality specific to Chinese thought (its concreteness, its constant preoccupation with the logic of the living and the social indistinct from an ontological preoccupation 'in itself'), Leibniz still fails to discover its essence when he reduces the heterogeneity of the *Li* (form and content at once) and its dichotomy (earth and heaven, life and death, man and woman, etc.) to the Cartesian principle of reason. From two opposite but converging directions the two philosophers manage to touch on the particularity of Chinese thought: the one to refuse it, the other to appropriate it for himself. But, together, and each in his own way, they fail to understand the essential problem that exists even in the Confucian texts and interpretations which the two are using: the problem of the *immanence* of 'reason' and 'matter', to such a point that there would be neither 'reason' nor 'matter' beyond their interdependence (which itself is the meaning of *Li*). The heterogeneous nature of this *Li* defies symbolism, and is actualized only by derivation, through a combination of opposing signs ($+$ and $-$, earth and sky, etc.), all of which are of equal value. In other words, there is no single isolatable symbolic principle to oppose itself and assert itself as transcendent law. It seems hardly an accident that this *immanence* was conceived by a society whose first family model is so marked by matrilinear descent and by the alteration of the two sexes, without an isolated symbolic authority aside from the principle of genitality and the economic/territorial contract. Quite a problem for our social theorists: is it a matter of simple determinism, of a 'reflection', an 'isomorphism' between, on the one hand, the relationships of production and reproduction and, on the other, the theoretical constructs? I can only ask the question here, and suggest that the intermediary point between these two terms may be found only in the actual situation of a (speaking) individual developing in such a sexo-economic structure and inevitably producing such an ideology. An individual, thus, that our fathers here — Jesuit or not — have trouble understanding. In any case, Chinese materialism (and perhaps all materialism that is not simply the inverse of idealism) could not be imagined outside a sexual and social economy where a woman, a mother, would assume her role as 'other' in a positive and unrepressed genitality.

The other essential characteristic of the Chinese universe is the system of writing, designed for a tonal language. This system of communication is certainly the first thing in China to strike the foreigner's ear and eye, and attract his attention. Linguists know that Chinese functions like any other language, that it is capable of transmitting messages without ambiguity. Modern theoreticians of transformational grammar are trying with some success to formulate the rules of Chinese grammar by making them conform to those of universal reason. Let's not even consider classical Chinese and the various poetic genres that scramble the message, weaving it into numerous ellipses and condensations. In everyday language itself, the 'white language' (*bai hua*) used today, the first thing one is aware of is the role that tonalities play in differentiating meanings. The same thing happens in the all tonal languages, and supports the discoveries of certain psycholinguists, i.e. that tonal variations and intonations are the first elements of the acoustic world that children are able to grasp and reproduce. They are quickly forgotten in a milieu where the language is not based on tones; but children surrounded by tonal speech do retain them, and quite early on. Thus, Chinese children begin taking part in the code of social communication that is language at a much younger age (5 or 6 months) than children in other cultures, since they are capable so early of distinguishing the fundamental trait of their language. And, as the dependency on the mother's body is so great at that age, it is thus the psycho-corporeal imprint of the mother that shapes tonal expression and transmits it without obliterating it, as the underlying but active stratum of communication. The grammatical system, on the other hand, will be a secondary acquisi-

55

tion, more 'socializing' because it insures the transmission of a message composed of meanings (and not only tonal impulses) to people other than thé mother. Does the Chinese language preserve, then, thanks to its tones, a pre-Oedipal, pre-syntactic, pre-symbolic (symbol and syntax being concomitant) register, even if it is evident that the tonal system is not fully realized except in syntax (like the phonological system in French, for example)?

The same question may be asked with regard to the writing. It is, at least in part — and at its origin — an imagistic writing; but it has become increasingly stylized, ideogrammatic, abstract. Nevertheless, it maintains its 'character', which is evocative both visually (in that it resembles an object or objects underlying an idea) and physically (because, to one who writes in Chinese, a memory for movement is more important than a memory for meaning). May we consider these visual and physical components to be manifestations of a psychic stratum more archaic even than those of sense and meaning, let alone logical and syntactical abstraction? As products of the vast unconscious storehouse from which the individual, thus, would never be cut off? It is accepted knowledge among modern historians and archaeologists that the great systems of writing (Egyptian, Babylonian, and Mayan, among others) were invented by the great 'despots'; as a means of centralizing power, perpetuating severe forms of slavery, carrying out great 'projects of state' (principally hydraulic), and developing a bureaucracy of religious or secular castes. If such, according to research, is the nature of productive relations in the great civilizations, we still know very little about the reproductive relations. The logic of Chinese writing (a visual representation, the mark of a gesture, a signifying arrangement of symbols, logic, and certain syntax) presupposes, at its base, a speaking, writing individual for whom what seems to us today a pre-Oedipal phase — dependency on the maternal, socio-natural continuum, absence of clear-cut divisions between the order of things and the order of symbols, predominance of the unconscious impulses — must have been extremely important. Ideogrammic or ideographic writing uses the characteristics of this phase for the ends of national, political, and symbolic

3.   Three generations of Chinese women. Photo taken around 1920.

4. A feminine brigade of Taoist guerrillas from Taiping.

5. Li Fenglan.

6. Her painting *The Harvest*: 'An old Taoist painter who dreams of being Van Gogh before waking to find himself a woman in a popular commune'.

7. Dance, music, writing: the girls enter with ease into the spirit of the times.

8. A teacher at Nanking: the peaceful open centre around which revolves the world of children and men.

power, *without censuring them.* A despotic power that has not forgotten what it owes to the mother and the matrilinear family that has certainly preceded it, though not by long. Hypothesis? Fantasy? — In any case, this would supplement an explanation of the disappearance of the great writing cultures in the face of the rise of monotheism and under its tread. After Egypt, Babylon, and the Mayans, only China (and its followers in Japan and southeast Asia) continues to 'write'. The structure of this system of social communication can perhaps be added to the list of historic and geographic accidents responsible for this fact. Not only has Chinese writing maintained the memory of matrilinear pre-history (collective and individual) in its architectonic of image, gesture, and sound; it has been able as well to integrate it into a logico-symbolic code capable of ensuring the most direct, 'reasonable', legislating — even the most bureaucratic — communication: all the qualities that the West believes itself unique in honouring, and that it attributes to the Father. We will return to these feudal and imperial acquisitions later on. Let us say simply here that the imposition of the 'symbolic instance' — *logical* in what concerns language, *despotic* when it comes to social and political matters — has never succeeded in eliminating the (logically) earlier stratum.

But the tones and the writing are not the only evidence that this stratum actively persists: a sort of reticence in meta-language , in the great metaphysical and/or philosophical theoretical systems, testifies to it as well. This reticence is responsible, perhaps, in another way, for something in the way that ancient and modern Chinese have of explaining their problems, which often is disconcerting to us. Rather than proceeding to an explanation which, for us, is the only logical one — which seeks the causes, makes the deductions, specifies the motivations, appearances, and essences, and at the same time foresees the consequences of an event — an operation which derives from the principle of a logical metaphysical causality — the Chinese give us a 'structuralist' or 'warring' (contradictory) portrait. Behind the event itself there appears a combinatorium or an association that bears the seed of the overthrow of the previous order; a battle between good and

57

evil; two-faced people: persecutions, conspiracies, sensational turns of event. As if the causal, deterministic metaphysical logic had crumbled before the traumatic occurrence whose advent we question; but without losing the symbolic level, the Chinese-speaking individual describes this event as if he were speaking of a game, a war, a combinatorium. We must add that the dramatic combinatorium that replaces the *principio reddendae rationis* is rife with allusions (which, of course, are beyond our comprehension) to historic or literary events familiar to any Chinese, without his necessarily being a scholar. So that it suffices to establish a structural analogy between the present circumstance and one in antiquity, which will eliminate the need to ask if and when the present event actually occurred: certainly it occurred, since it is being made analogous to an event that is certified by literature and tradition. Such an 'aesthetic' mode of reasoning may make us uneasy; but it has a certain symbolic effectiveness. By eliminating straight away the problem of an 'objective truth' (which it would be imposs-ible to do in the political world burdened with power relation-ships), it shifts people to a symbolic situation in literature or in the past, selected according to the influence it continues to exert in the present. And it is there, in that symbolic, arche-typal situation, that the dramas of passion, ideology, and politics that underlie the present traumatic event which con-cerns us and which we seek to understand (in our own terms) are called into play and begin to unravel, as in a psychodrama, a pre-psychoanalytic 'happening'; as in the sort of theatre Sade introduced for the inmates at Charenton.

A revival of archaic, pre-Oedipal modes of operation? A con-sonance with the very latest methods of logic and psychology? In any case, it is also, perhaps, this kind of thinking that ties ancient to modern China, the old semi-feudal society to com' munism. It is also, perhaps, what separates us from any Chinese man or woman with whom we enter into dialogue . . . across Huxian Square.

I went to the Panpo Museum of pre-history, near Xi'an. The excavations begun in 1953 have unearthed a village that modern Chinese archeologists consider to have been organized as a primitive matriarchal commune, prior to the appearance of patriarchy, private property, and class distinctions. In 1958, the findings were placed in a museum which, by a state decree of 1961, is under the auspices of the State Council. A woman of about thirty, who looked like a suntanned schoolgirl, told us about ancient times. Chang Shufang, mother of two, did not study history at the University. She began by teaching herself in whatever time she had left over from her more or less technical duties as museum guide, and she is presently continuing her studies in night classes, where university professors come to teach museum employees. Chang Shufang among the ruins of Panpo: a veritable dramatic setting of Engels' *On the Origin of the Family, Private Property, and The State*. The ruins of this 8,000-year-old village are spread over a territory of about 16 acres: the relics in the museum come from the two and a half acres that have been explored to date. Three distinct zones arise on this soil, whitened by time and limestone, creating before my eyes the distant life which Mme Chang attempts to explain with the help of Engels.

There are two types of habitation: round ones above ground, and square ones slightly below the surface. Do they indicate a separation of sexes (men, women)? Different practical uses (homes, silos)? Or different historical periods? Seed fossils — millet, colza, wild plants — suggest a certain level of agricultural development: 'It was the women who gathered the wild plants; by cultivating them around the house, women invented agriculture, which allowed them to play a major social — and even political — role,' explains Mme Chang. 'Men devoted themselves to hunting and fishing, and, later on, to breeding animals.' The village, along the banks of the River Zhanhe, abounded in fish. The fish was a totem, and is represented in pottery paintings. At the centre of the village was the house of the Great Ancestress, surrounded by hearths where men and women belonging to the two divisions of the economy (farmers and hunters) gathered together at night. Outside the village, separated by a sort of moat were the two other areas, burial grounds and pottery works, side by side. There are round vessels made of terra cotta, of variable size (from five to thirty cm), widening at the mouth, with or without a spout. Some have inscriptions — the precursors of writing? — trac-

59

ings, runes, auguries. Others are covered with elegant designs in black and red-brown: fish, pairs of fish, or simply squares, circles, and triangles which, according to Chang Shufang, are earlier representations of fish. But there are also wild birds, elephants, giraffes, who don't seem to have lived in the region: are they the fruit of some imagination, or the memories of migrants? In any case, one finds the impressions of women's fingernails on the pottery. Women not only cultivated the grain, but made the pottery and did the cooking. Some of the pottery is hand-cast, some seems to have been thrown on a wheel. A pot made for drawing water demonstrates a certain empirical knowledge of the laws of gravity. One pot uses steam for cooking. All are evidence, according to Chang Shufang, of the development of production in the primitive commune.

We know that it was matriarchal essentially from the burial grounds. The women's graves contain more funerary objects — pottery, bracelets, bone hairpins, whistles, etc. — than the men's. Children are buried with the women (only babies are not admitted to the burial ground; their bodies are placed in urns not far from the houses). Here, there are common graves: men are buried with men, and women with women. But in this same region of Xi'an, another excavation has revealed the existence of burial grounds where the Mother occupies the central position, and is surrounded by the skeletons of the other members of the 'family' (doubtless a two-part funeral rite: first the two sexes are buried in separate graves, then the family is placed around the grandmother). Sacrificial rites do not appear to have been among the customs of this period, and, therefore, of the matriarchal commune: none of the skeletons bears evidence of a violent death. Finally, according to Mme Chang, the central house, the Great Ancestress' house, seems to have been also the central meeting place, where the political affairs of this society without paternal domination or private property were collectively decided. Recent paintings illustrate the conclusions of Chang Shufang. One sees the Great Ancestress, whose youthful features seem more Ukranian than Chinese, directing the groups of hunters, potters, and farmers. In a recent speech, Mao himself seems deeply persuaded of her existence:

(In primitive society) there was not yet the practice of burying women with their dead husbands, but they were obliged to subject themselves to men. First men were subject to women, and then things moved towards their opposite, and women were subject to men. This stage in history has not yet been clarified, although it has been going on for a million years and more. Class society has not yet lasted 5,000 years. Cultures such as that of Lung Shan and Yang Shao at the end of the primitive era had coloured pottery. In a word, one devours another, one overthrows another . . .[1]

A fantasy projection of some Golden Age? An accidental coincidence of Engels' theories and the Chinese past? A superficial interpretation of archeological facts? Perhaps. But the enigma persists: a mother at the centre.

Is it an echo of this central role of the tribal mother that we hear in the sexual treatises and erotic rites of feudal China? What is certain is that all the manuals of the 'Art of the Bed-chamber' — which date back to the first century A.D. — depict the woman as the principal initiator of love-making, since it is she who knows not only its technique, but also its secret (alchemical) meaning and its benefits to the body (longevity). Furthermore, she is portrayed as the party whose right to *jouissance* is incontestable. Thus, the three female figures who, in the form of a dialogue that is anything but platonic, teach the arcane meanings of sex to the Emperor: Shunü (Daughter of Candour), Xuannü (Daughter with Jade Hair), and Cainü (Chosen Daughter), quite obviously know a great deal more than the males who come to consult them — before the 'masters' of later treatises come along and cloak amorous advice in military terminology. But whether it is divulged by a woman or an expert 'master', the advice about love-making is principally concerned with the pleasure of the woman. Foreplay is extensively discussed, and the goal of the act itself, each

---

[1]"Discourse on Philosophical Problems, August 18, 1964," in Mao Tse-tung, *Unrehearsed Talks and Letters: 1956-74*, edited by Stuart Schram, Pelican Books, 1974. P.226.

time, is the orgasm of the woman, who is thought to have an inexhaustible *yin* essence, whereas the man, on the other hand, the delicate artisan of this *jouissance,* is supposed to withold his own orgasm in order to achieve health and longevity, if not immortality. One can imagine social reasons for such practices: polygamy required a certain order in the relationships among the various wives, and demanded that they be satisfied at least at regular intervals so that peace reigned in the harem; obviously, the one available male had to spare his strength. Whatever the reasons, though, the psychosomatic result of this kind of *jouissance* is that the woman does not consider herself as 'inferior', 'devalued', and desirable only at that price — which is the case in sexual economies dominated by the phallus. Furthermore, because the man is neither the master nor the active, inducing principle of the orgasm, but rather one of two who are each two in themselves (each partner being both *male* and *female,* the difference between them being a matter of degree), the sexual act becomes a mutual exchange: what is missing in the one is offered by the other. Without being an 'egalitarianism' — since it maintains the differences — this kind of sexual practice is essentially genital: the sexual treatises are designed for married life. They impress us with their positivity, their attitude toward sex as 'normal': nothing is sinful in this refined quest for pleasure. What we think of as perversion seems to integrate itself easily into these customs: female homosexuality in particular. A vestige of the 'matriarchy' or the *modus vivendi* of the polygamous family? Female sexuality and masturbation are not merely 'tolerated' — they are taken for granted and considered to be perfectly 'natural'. Sexual treatises provide detailed descriptions of lesbian and masturbatory techniques, some of them extraordinarily sophisticated. What *is* problematic is the woman who cheats: the one who tries to pass for a man, who perverts the *yin/yang* duality by acting as a rather brutal, domineering male seducer. Male homosexuality seems more problematic, even though during certain periods (the earlier Han, who reigned in the early centuries B.C., and, also, particularly, the southern Song Dynasty, 1127-1279; but also the Ming — 1368-1644) it was practised quite openly, and underlay what were called the 'great intellectual friendships' under the Tang (618-906). But, without being isolated as a 'special case', a 'deviation', or a 'sexual peculiarity', homosexuality seems about as diffuse in the vast current of genital eroticism as sadism and masochism. Van Gulik[1] emphasizes that cases of 'perversion' are rare in China. It might be more accurate to say that they are rare as such, in isolation; but the so-called 'perverted' act is incorporated into an erotic practice where whatever is pleasurable is considered 'normal', provided that the pleasure includes, at one point or another in the process, *both sexes*. One can *engage* in homosexual, sadistic or masochistic practises; one *is not defined as* a sadist, a masochist, a homosexual.

Such an economy, based on the *jouissance* of the woman without sacrificing that of the man, proceeds from the idea that the sexual relationship is not a relationship of identification, absorption of the one by the other, negation of the differences. In other words, nothing in the sexual-psychological relationship here corresponds to the western medieval concept of love. The explosive, blossoming, sane and inexhaustible *jouissance* of the woman is perhaps precisely that permanent flight which precludes two individuals, two psychic entities, from coming together to gaze narcissistically into each other's eyes. But this feminine *jouissance*, that could become the support of the mystery, the ultimate source of God, the Absolute, does not do so in China; for it is constantly counterbalanced by the other, the *yang*, which certainly takes for itself and gives of itself, but not every time. The *yang* represents the limit of *jouissance*, the prohibition that may be ephemeral, may be overridden — but is nonetheless present. It is precisely this difference, this *otherness*, which is brought back into balance after the act of love; and precisely because the two terms are well separated, without possibility of confusion. Some praise it, others regret it. A melancholy regret, that draws strength from the fact that women, high priestesses of carnal love, are excluded from social relationships and become alienated in a feudal society whose hierarchical order depends on forgetting

---

[1] *La vie sexuelle dans la Chine ancienne*, Gallimard 1971.

the bedchamber.

> They who were first as form and shadow
> Now they are distant as Chinese and Huns.
> Even Chinese and Huns meet now and then,
> While husband and wife are as different as Lucifer
> and Orion.

writes Fu Xian in the third century A.D. But praise is heard
from others, because if men and women are two separate races
and even two separate universes, their conflict is an aspect of
the perpetual cosmic and social movement. This permanent flux
has no 'unity' save that of *conception,* which has nothing
immaculate or universally stable about it, but rather takes
place during a complex strategy between two sexes. Such a
strategy cannot be defined; it can only be suggested by metaphor: the alchemical crucible, or war.

> On the incarnation of the Tao, the true Oneness (i.e. con-
> ception) is difficult to represent. After this transmutation,
> the couple separates, and each one returns again to his
> or her own side.[1]

Much emphasis has been placed on the influence of Chinese
sexual theory and practice on the development of the sexual
mystique of Tantric Buddhism. There is one essential difference, however, between the Chinese universe and the Buddhist
universe in this regard: in China, the two sexes harmonize,
but generally do not fuse. The erotic-alchemical dyad of
Taoism is not a hermaphrodite; never does the one absorb the
other to the point that its existence is made superfluous. The
Tantra, on the other hand, says: 'Why should I need another
woman? I have a woman within myself.' Taoism nourishes this
concept of sexual life that underlies Chinese society, and
remains permanently in the shadow of family life, even when
Confucianism reigns supreme over the political scene from at
least the Song period on. Taoist sects, and, afterward, Taoist
institutions (like Buddhist monasteries) are reputed to have

---

[1]According to the Taoist treatise on alchemy: *The Pact of the
Triple Equation,* quoted by Van Gulik, p. 115.

given refuge to sexual practices where women played the major role, when such practices were condemned by Confucian propaganda. Later on, we shall see the extent to which women were despised in some forms of Confucianism; but even these never had the idea of 'carnal sin', and certain Taoist precepts were integrated into the system during the Confucian revival of the eleventh century. However, without proscribing eroticism, Confucianism began by subordinating it to the goal of procreation. Like some of our contemporary anthropologists, the Confucians were interested only in those aspects of sexual practice that would insure procreation. They would later embark on an all-out attack on the sex manuals of the Han and the Tang, and would prohibit any demonstration of heterosexual relationship. Finally, during the Ming Dynasty (1368-1644), they would plunge into an embittered puritanism where eroticism became a deviation, a transgression, reserved for bordellos and for what henceforth would be known as pornographic literature.

What's left today of the 'Art of the Bedchamber' and its feminine *jouissance*? What's left of the treatises of the Han and the Tang after Confucian puritanism and the modern importation of bourgeois morality?

A secret sect, practising group sex according to Taoist rules, was dissolved in 1950.

A more or less Confucian 'modesty' is still in evidence. Is this a result of the effort at sublimation required to build the new society? Or is it simply distrust of strangers? It is impossible to get the Chinese to talk about it today. But one can watch these relaxed feminine bodies floating lightly along the streets of Peking, among the tufts of willow moss. One can glimpse the quick, hot, laughing glances, or the clever, furtive smiles of these girls, walking arm-in-arm through the park. Or one can listen to these women's voices, which don't stick in the throat, but rather vibrate, rhythmic and melodious, with the whole body, down to the tiniest cell, free of guilt or provocation. An empty centre, around which the society of men revolves without ever speaking of it. So . . . one can think what one pleases, before these people. Beginning with oneself.

65

II

Confucius—An Eater of Women

This is not the place to join the highly technical and confused discussions of sinologists and anthropologists on the various forms of kinship in China. After Granet, Feng, Hsu, Lévi-Strauss and others, the givens are still contradictory or insufficient to suggest new interpretations, even to a specialist, which I am not. But even the evolutionist, functionalist, and structuralist methodologies, which might be able to guide us in making interpretations, do not take women and women's point of view into account in their discussion of the rules of kinship. And it is not at all impossible that these rules might appear altogether different to us if we observed them from the point of view of the losers. So it's up to women sinologists and women anthropologists to see. . . . Let us say simply that the two family models in China have nothing exclusively Chinese about them; that they may be encountered in other parts of the world; but it is in China that they seem to achieve their highest development. It is interesting too that they are found in the (numerically) greatest civilization in the modern world, a civilization which is highly stable politically and which has made its entrance into the modern arena with surprising energy. Let us examine the most schematic and least debatable aspects of these two models in question, and the transition (structural or historic) from one to the other. The first model, which we have described as *matrilinear* and *matrilocal* and based on *peasant custom*, was founded on the rules of a restricted exchange between two exogamous groups separated along sexual/economic/territorial lines. In all probability, descent was bilateral: one could marry one's cousin on the father's or the mother's side. Thus, the children retained the local name of the mother, or added to it (perhaps later on) the family name of the father. Chinese parental nomenclature supports this hypothesis that bilateral descent was the rule prior to the unilateral paternal descent which was later instituted. Thus, it seems, Engels' 'matriarchy' and the first communal family model attested to by peasant chants and legends (alternation of sexes and 'professional corporations') boil down to the rules of restricted exchange and bilateral descent. In any case, anthropology can say so without too much recourse to fiction.

The restricted exchange between two exogamous halves of the clan implied not only the exchange of women, but also (since the basic social division exerted an influence on all levels of kinship) the exchange of girl cousins of mixed (bilateral) descent (matrilateral *and* patrilateral). However, another form of marriage consists in a male individual marrying only his cousin on his mother's side, the daughter of his mother's brother. From here on in we are in a simple generalized exchange, patrilinear and patrilocal, with its common corollary, polygamy. Before this, the Chinese system is matrilinear and matrilocal. The new type of marriage is coextensive with a feudalistic society: by admitting the possibility not only of exchanging, but of buying wives, it favours the wealthier classes and creates a social hierarchy. This type of marriage, the product of wife-buying and of a simple generalized exchange (marriage with one or more maternal cousins) will be borrowed by Confucianism, the ritualizer of feudalism. By dropping some of its elements (marriage with one's cousin, for example) and preserving others (wife-buying), it will arrive at a free exchange and, at the same time, a political and economic hierarchy.

The first revolution of the Chinese family, which we spoke of above, lies precisely in the introduction of the simple generalized exchange, where the male Ego cannot marry the daughters of aunts on his father's side, but only the daughters of his maternal uncles. On the other hand, one may consider this generalized exchange as an elementary type of marriage by exchange, a modified variant of the phenomenon of reciprocity that is fundamental to the logic of any marriage; and, therefore, as the simple, logical consequence of an eternal anthropological structure. Such a position would be more structuralist, more rigourously logical, and would eliminate the problem of the historical evolution of forms of marriage, and approach, rather, a Biblical conception (in the sense we discussed earlier). Above all, it would eliminate the need to concern ourselves with a previous social order, where an individual (necessarily male) is not yet the organizing principle of the social system, and consequently, where the politics (or whatever took the place of politics) are not necessarily paternal, with women as objects of exchange. Conversely, if we resolve to postulate the logical possibility of a politics that was not egalitarian, but rather hetero-logical, including both sexes, and where the structurally necessary role of 'object of exchange' was not necessarily always assumed by women, and where the Ego was not yet considered as such, we might well begin to believe that marriage with the first cousin on the mother's side is a transitional form between matrilinear and matrilocal restricted exchange and the agnatic family.

This radical, if not abrupt, transformation puts a quick end to the Dynasty of Matrons, the endogamous community with two exogamous groups. It eliminates, thus, the maternal line of descent that is evident in the restricted exchange: since in this first system one can marry any cousin (male or female) descended from 'another mother', because whether one considers him/her 'the same as oneself' (endogamous) or 'another' (exogamous) depends on whether the prospective spouse has the same maternal lineage. This system of intra-clan 'exogamy' was still vigorously alive under Zhou Gong, in 1100 B.C. But with the new reforms that seem to have been made around 1000 B.C. and were sanctioned by law between 1000-500 B.C., the *agnatic family* (and with it, a strict exogamy) replaces the two *exogamous groups* of the endogamous clans. The Order of the Fathers replaces the Order of the Mothers, and the importance of the maternal uncle may be seen as a transitional step towards the patrilinear — and later patriarchal — institution

68

of Confucianism. This form of kinship known as simple generalized exchange according to which, in a system of patrilinear or matrilinear descent, the individual marries his matrilateral cousin and no one else, is evident even in the names of kinship terms and funeral rituals (among others, the celebrated *zhao mu* order — according to which the fathers *[zhao]* and sons *[mu]* belong to different categories, but grandfathers and grandsons, to the same). It seems also that, by means of certain transformations which we cannot elaborate on here, this system gives rise to a sort of 'legalized incest': marriage with the father's widow, with the widow or the fiancée of the son, or with the daughter of the wife's brother. But some traces of the earlier model (restricted bilateral exchange) remain: a preference for marriage to the daughter of the mother's brother persists in certain regions of China until after the Second World War. It is worth noting that Confucian morality, which sought, among other things, to eliminate all traces of matrilinear descent, was forced to fight against marriage between bilateral cousins and with the daughter of the mother's brother, and at the same time to accord it a certain place within the accepted body of law. Thus, marriage between crossed bilateral cousins is prohibited in the first century A.D.; but, much later, the Code of the Ming (1368-1644) re-institutes this prohibition, indicating that common practice was still to the contrary. And during the Qing (1644-1912) the Code begins by prohibiting it and ends up authorizing it 'in the public interest'.

Granet suggests that between the two family models — bilateral matrilinear descent with four classes, and unilateral descent by marriage with the daughter of the maternal uncle, paving the way for the modern patriarchal, patrilinear system of 'free exchange' — there was a period of transition characterized, among other things, by the introduction of an additional prohibition: the stratification of generations and a taboo on mariage outside one's age-group. A highly controversial system of eight classes is thus proposed by the sinologist to account for this transition. This law against cross-generational marriage was so frequently transgressed that, in the sixth century, a Tang code re-legislates it into being. It seems, however, that the nobility continued to ignore it.

The essential problem that the existence of these two family models in China (matrilinear descent/agnatic family) poses for us is to determine whether the one evolved from the other, or whether we are dealing with two entirely different structural types. Granet seems to lean toward a mixed response: restricted exchange with bilateral matrilinear descent is peculiar to the peasantry, while a patrilinear family with matrilateral descent (marriage with the daughter of the maternal uncle) is found first among the wealthy classes and the nobility. But even if there were two different structures belonging to the two economically (and perhaps also ethnically) different levels of society, some type of evolution still took place to produce the second model, the one common to the nobility. Such an evolution would be due to the increasing importance of the father/son relationship, probably dictated, ultimately, by economic reasons (the development of agriculture and stock-farming, which required a commitment of time and a physical strength that mothers could not furnish; also, the development of trades and crafts that had the same requirements), but by political reasons as well (periods of war, organization of trades and military castes). The development of the cult of ancestor-worship is certainly another factor in this *evolution, which, in relation to the previous model, marks an indisputable historical progression.*

The worship of the spirits of dead ancestors is evidence of the fact that a symbolic community (no longer only sexual, economic, or territorial) is being built, whose cohesion or unity is insured by its descent from a common ancestry, and whose contact with the life of the unit or the individual is entirely abstract. Confucianism will be founded precisely on this cult of ancestor worship, finding in it a solid base for the construction of a rationalist morality with a strong paternal authority and a complex hierarchy. A family based on free exchanges (in which, however, the preference for marriage with one's cousins still persists) will establish itself under the incontestable authority of the ancestors, the father, and the eldest son. By contrast, in the peripheral societies (Tibetan, Burman, Siberian) which, after being expelled by the Han, became nomadic and lost the relative stability of the agrarian peasant society of central China, one finds a certain tendency toward the return of the simple generalized exchange between two exogamous groups distinguished by the persistence of marriage with the daughter of the maternal uncle.

What are the chief characteristics of the Confucian family, which follows the earlier agnatic family and dominates China until the Liberation in 1949, and against whose surviving influence a tremendous campaign (*Pi Lin Pi Kong*) is currently being waged?

The contract drawn up between families of different names (so as to insure exogamy) survives in the form of the buying and selling of daughters, often from early childhood. Marriage is the business of the parents, who find suitable mates for their children. The future wife, then, may be one of her husband's childhood playmates; but her position is far inferior to his, as she is 'employed' to do the housework under the unquestionable authority of her mother-in-law. In wealthy families one marries a 'principal wife'; she comes along with a suite of concubines, who may be older or younger than herself, and may or may not be related to her. Such a group marriage creates intra-familial relationships rather than individual ones: in the eyes of her new family, a woman represents her original family or group, and thus assumes no role whatever for herself — personal, psychological, or otherwise. She cannot even be jealous of the other women if they come from the same family group as she does. Woman is the nomadic element of the society, as well as its dramatic element. Homeless even among her own family — who, knowing she is destined to leave them, never quite treat her as one of their own — she lives as a stranger in her adopted family, until her first male child is born and reaches maturity. A woman is submitted throughout her life to a whole series of authorities: her own mother and father, her husband's mother and father, her husband, and, finally, her son. The wedding and engagement rituals symbolize just that state of distance and even warfare which reigns in such 'contractual' families: the crossing of the thresholds of the two houses, the carrying of the bride to the ceremony on the bridal chair, the humility of the husband before his wife's family, the humility of the wife before her husband's family, the observation of the wedding night by attendants of both bride and groom, the 'trial period' after the wedding during which separation of the couple is not considered a divorce, etc. Several taboos — the wife must not speak to the husband; the couple must not hang their clothing in the same place — are also indicative of this state of provisional truce between two adversary — if not warring — groups, which is the feudal family.

The ancient feudal family, but also the one known to us in the twentieth century, is more ritualistic among the wealthy, and closer to peasant tradition in the countryside. This family — the *jia* — is not only a union of individuals bound to each other by blood ties. It is 'an economic family', i.e. a unit constituted of members connected by blood, marriage, or adoption, and having a common budget and common property.[1] Thus, the *jia* groups together people who, on the basis of blood ties and marriage, live above all as an 'economic unit': in this case, they may be natural families, or families who have not yet subdivided their ancestral heritage and live together with that heritage representing their chief symbolic and economic tie. Without attempting an analysis of the highly complex economic structure of the *jia*, and without speaking of the 'religious families' or other conventional families which are agnatic groupings but outside domestic life, let us say that, since it is essentially an economic notion, a family can continue to form a unit even when its members are scattered in various parts of the country or abroad.[2]

The right to give orders falls to the father. It is interesting, though, to note that the father does not derive his authority from the fact of being sire, but rather because he belongs to the lineage of ancestors. His son reveres him because he sees in him a potential ancestor. In a survival of the system of

---

[1]Olga Lang, *Chinese Family and Society*, New Haven, 1946.

[2]Myron L. Cohen, 'Developmental Process in the Chinese Domestic Group', in *Family and Kinship in Chinese Society*, edited by Maurice Freedman, Stanford Univ. Press, California, 1970.

maternal right and bilateral descent, the son does not belong to his father's group: the father is *yang* and the son *yin*, the father *zun* (respectable) and *yan* (severe, remote), but not *qin* (close). Paternity is not necessarily based on the birth of a child from a genetic mother and father. A man can confer his paternity on a child he has not sired, and, conversely, refuse it to a child he has sired. A 'rite of bonding' or 'admission', a second birth, is required to place the child under the paternal regime. This ritual generally takes place at the moment when the child is thought to possess a soul (*hun*), which does not come to him from his mother, but which, three months after his birth, is apparent in his laugh, or may be precociously awakened by a musician if the musician has felt particularly sensitive to the infant's earliest cries. The presentation of the child to the father consecrates his passage into the paternal order, like an initiation rite or a military induction ceremony. However, the child returns to 'the women's side' and sees neither his father nor any other man until his seventh year. After this point, his education is undertaken by a man from the maternal family (survival of the right of the maternal uncle) where the child is sent to be taken care of. Later, the father and son continue to be thought of as belonging to two different sexes, or as sexual rivals for the possession of the widow or fiancée. Once he is grown up, educated, and married (at about thirty, the son, if he is an older son, becomes the first vassal of the parental couple, and acts as their minister, managing family affairs with the help of his own principal wife. The respect and obedience due to the father are evident as well in the very strict duties of mourning which the son must perform for a long period after his father's death. After that, it is the eldest son who becomes the uncontested head of the *jia;* and it appears that he may do so to an increasing degree even during his father's lifetime, once his father has passed the age of sixty. Let us insist as well on the fact that this symbolic (and not genetic) paternal authority is considered to be something that distinguishes humans from other animals, and is praised as a proof of civilization. Then again, the father embodies at once the functions of symbolic authority and the qualities of woman: he is 'the father and the mother', gentle and severe, authoritarian, but not punitive. In the imagination of the culture, the symbolic father dispossesses the mother of her maternity, and thus, of her role in the social balance. By appropriating this role, he tends to put an end to the alternation of the two sexes that characterized the first matrilinear and bilateral family model. We can make many observations on this phenomenon; but perhaps the most concise is found in the famous Chinese adage:

> Animals know their mother and not their father. Peasants say mother and father are the same. But the noblemen in the city honour their dead fathers.

Insofar as the Father will one day die (and only then assume his full stature in the ranks of the dead ancestors), he becomes the support of an authority that obliterates the difference between the sexes, and, in the same blow, censures the function of genitality in the sexual economy of the society.

Commenting on the effects of the Confucian family on individual psychology, Francis L. K. Hsu writes: 'As far as the overt behaviour (of an individual brought up under these conditions) is concerned, the first outstanding quality is an explicitly submissive attitude toward authority. . . . There are very few choices and few uncertainties. All routes are, so to speak, barred, except one, that which follows the footsteps of his father, his father's father, and the whole line of his more remote ancestors.'[1]

If what he says is true, we can understand the stakes and the ambition involved in the current campaign against the Old Sage. It must do no more and no less than transform the mental structure of the Chinese, and make him something other than Chinese.

In this order, a woman's role is as the object over whom authority is exercised. Daughters, those nomads, those perpetual strangers in the feudal and Confucian systems, are not entitled to the rite of bonding and paternal adoption.

---

[1]Francis L. K. Hsu, *Under the Ancestor's Shadow*, New York, Columbia Univ. Press, 1948, p. 260.

They belong to the gynaecium, and leave it only to join another household. They are subjected to the mother, insofar as she represents paternal authority; absolute piety and obedience to the family is demanded of them, and they remain forever bound to their original household because they bear its name even once they have taken on the yoke of the parents-in-law and the husband. And yet, oddly enough, it does not seem that they are as strictly compelled to revere their own fathers as are their brothers. A certain familiarity exists between father and daughter, different from the 'distance' and 'severity' between father and son. But if this relative relaxation of paternal discipline allows the daughter a bit more room, it signifies, at the same time, the total disregard of her in the order of males who are potential (dead) ancestors. Confucius put women in the same class as 'slaves', 'xiao ren', 'inferior men'. This treatment, which goes along with the oppression of women under the hierarchy of authorities in the feudal family, earned Confucius the name of 'eater of women', among all those who, on various grounds, have fought against his influence on Chinese social custom.

Among all the sayings attributed to Confucius, we find only one definition of women:

> It is not pleasing to have to do with women or people of base condition. If you show them too much affection, they become too excited, and if you keep them at a distance, they are full of resentment. (*Lun yu*, chap. XVII)

Hardly a false estimation when it comes to controlling matters of psychology, but it's backed by a whole moral code of paternal piety, where women are, at best, passed over in silence. Cloistered in their houses, *nei ren* ('humans for the inside'), they are, according to Confucianism, destined only for housework and reproduction. Consequently, there is no need for them to learn to read and write. The arts — poetry, drawing, singing — don't have to be learned except by the 'ladies of the night', the various categories of courtesans who are employed less for the pleasures of the body than for the joys of aesthetic conversation.

So, with Confucianism, two barriers are erected to insure the cohesion of the feudal social order: the first is the door to the bedchamber, the second is writing and knowledge in general. A woman cannot cross them both at once: either she leaves the bedchamber to be acknowledged — but only as genetrix — the mother of the father's sons; or she gains access to the social order (as poet, dancer, singer) but behind the door of the bedchamber, an unacknowledgeable sexual partner. Only the man will be entitled to sexual pleasures, paternity, and all the forms of symbolic sublimation. By this double bind in which women are held, the society protects itself from the *jouissance* that can drive it to madness or revolution: it keeps itself stable, permanent, eternal. Yang Chen, a famous Confucianist of the Han Dynasty (d. A.D. 124), goes straight to the point:

> If women are given work that requires contact with the outside, they will sow disorder and confusion throughout the Empire. Shame and injury will come to the Imperial Court, and the Sun and the Moon (Emperor and Empress) will wither away. The Book of Documents warns us against the hen who announces the dawn in place of the rooster; the Book of Odes denounces a clever woman who overthrows a State . . . Women must not be allowed to participate in the affairs of the government.[1]

Let us quote a few more of the numerous Confucian texts which insist on the inferiority of women:

> When a newborn baby comes into the world, if it's a boy as strong as a wolf, his parents are still afraid that he might be too weak; whereas if it's a girl as sweet and as gentle as a little mouse, her parents still fear she might be too strong. (Han Shu)

> Give a woman an education and all you will get from her is boredom and complaints. (Sima Guang, Song Dynasty)

---

[1]Cited by Van Gulik, p.121.

In addition, Confucian poetic convention requires that man/ woman relationships be the metaphor for lord/vassal relationships, and vice-versa. Not an innocent rhetorical device. We can appreciate the irony in Mao's comments on it:

> Confucius, too was rather democratic, he included (in the *Book of Odes*) poems about the love between man and woman. In his commentaries, Chu Hsi characterized them as poems about clandestine love affairs. In reality, some of them are and some of them aren't; the latter borrow the imagery of man and woman to write about the relations between prince and subject. In Shu (present-day Szechwan) at the time of the Five Dynasties and Ten Countries, there was a poem entitled 'The Wife of Ch'in Laments the Winter', by Wei Chuang. He wrote it in his youth, and it is about his longing for his prince.[1]

Without a right to the human — i.e. male — hierarchy, and, consequently, largely without an education; condemned to endless humiliation if she is not a 'principal wife' and back-breaking labour when she doesn't belong to a wealthy family, woman is subjected as well to the internal rivalry within the female contingent of the family, which reflects in microcosm the power-structure in the male hierarchy. Internal rivalries between wives and concubines at various levels (first wife, second wife, etc.), but also between daughter-in-law and mother-in-law; or between sisters-in-law, where the war between the brothers for succession to the fathers is echoed. Although they are obliged to behave in certain ways, women are less bound to Confucian hypocrisy. Thus, in their own society, they give free rein to the impassioned violence that gnaws at the apparent interior harmony of the patriarchal class. Their arguments, shouts, even fistfights — let alone their plots and conspiracies — are celebrated in fiction, and by many observers. They reveal what lies under the floorboards of Confucianism; but, more importantly, they reveal the wretchedness of the female condition, and that accumulation of unused

---

[1]*Mao Tse-Tung Unrehearsed*, talks and letters: 1956-1971, edited by Stuart Schram, Pelican Books, 1974, p. 215.

impulses, capable of channelling themselves into merciless aggression and into intrigues of astonishing complexity. As more or less distant observers, men certainly were the benefactors of these feminine schemings; but that did not make them any less afraid of them; especially when, before the Liberation, thanks to a certain degree of female emancipation brought about by the bourgeoisie (which we'll discuss later on), we begin to see women leaving the household and taking up roles in society. Witnesses say that — whether from misogynist fantasies or from their own experience — men were afraid of the rise of these women, who were such specialists in violence and family intrigue. What could they expect from that repressed force, once it came into power, but more of the same? But even in this state of dependence or moralistic Confucian tyranny, survivals of bilateral descent and the intermediate form of simple generalized exchange requiring marriage with the daughter of the maternal uncle continue to grant women, under certain conditions, some way in which to escape being entirely crushed by the Law of the Fathers.

This is first of all because Confucius and Mencius are their mothers' sons. Confucius' father is unknown, but his mother plays an important role as his protector and his inspiration. Mencius' mother is even more famous for having procured for her son the favourable conditions he needed for his education. Confucianism, negligent or severe with regard to women, will not require anything of them except procreation. As happens elsewhere, it does not taint sexual relations with anything 'evil', but acknowledges them only for purposes of reproduction. There is no cult of the Virgin; the Mother (if she's not Confucius' mother) is in the shadows.

In a system of agnatic descent, and even in the Confucian family, the importance of the role of women, and, especially, of their parents, persists. It can become a dominant factor when a woman belongs to a rich and politically powerful family; but, in any case, it increases after she has passed the age of 'young errant girl' and 'mother/stranger' and she reigns as adult wife through her eldest son and becomes, on the death of her husband, the uncontested power in the family. A novel of the Qing Dynasty (which gives an accurate portrait of the mores of noble families and which is currently studied in China as evidence of the insoluble link between class struggle and intra/interfamilial attitudes), *The Dream of the Red Pavilion*, portrays the struggle of young Baoyu against paternal authority. It emphasizes at once the fragility and submissiveness of the young woman, and the omnipotence of the old mother. One is struck by the authoritarian — even virile — aspect of this power of the first-wife-become-grandmother-of-the-family. Granet suggests a rather attractive explanation: on the one hand, maternity in a feudal family is a collective and symbolic fact. The only mother is the first wife, and all the other wives' children are considered to be hers. Any other genetic mother has only nieces and nephews; though some of them may be children she has in fact, given birth to, their symbolic, authoritative, and only recognized mother is the first wife. As if, after having been stripped of maternal power, and of the social rights which such power conferred on her in the first family model (matrilineal descent), and after seeing this power and these rights assumed by in-laws and husband a woman in certain circumstances (first wife, rich, noble origin) could return to the front of the stage and reclaim her authority. But this time she will only *represent* the authority of the in-laws and the husband; she herself *is not* the authority, she herself is not vested with it, she is never 'herself'. Another reason for the 'virile' power of the grandmother: given the survival of the maternal right, a son has no value outside that of his maternal group. So he can eventually fight against his father with the support of his mother, but he can never fight against his mother (after the father's death, for example); for by so doing he would be ruining that very thing whose prestige he is — his base, his *raison d'être*. Thus, the feudal family, even when it reserves a place for the power of women (the elderly first wife or the widow) by making them homologous with the power of the father (is there any other?) leaves no possibility at all for the *other* sex to assume its role as *other* and to function as *other* in the productive and reproductive relations. The individual — man or woman — finds him/herself cornered in this system, on the one side by the power of the (dead) fathers, and on the other by the power of the grandmothers who reflect the sunlight of the ancestors like stubborn moons.

One might think, however, that, despite everything, the existence of two (unequal but nonetheless present) poles of familial power allows the desires (and, thus, the symbolizing capacity) of the individual a bit more room to manoeuvre than they have in the monotheistic, patriarchal family. Even if such an interpretation were true, it is undeniable that feudalism and Confucianism were used to impose the maximum patriarchal, ancestral, and symbolic authority; so that at the dawn of the bourgeois age in China, and of the revolution that followed it, the traditional family constitutes one of the chief obstacles to liberation, more difficult to overcome than even the western family at the height of its crisis.

The 'feminine power' — homologous especially in wealthy families to the power of the fathers — made it possible for Chinese women intellectuals raised in the West to identify with European suffragettes. It may still foster certain tendencies toward the virilization of women under the socialist regime. But, for one who wishes to analyze the specificity of the female body and the female function in patrilinear, patriarchal, productivist society, this 'power' serves as a screen, if not an insurmountable barrier.

Other aspects of this 'feminine power' in the feudal family emphasize its ambiguous nature even more.

With the exception of the rites celebrated in honour of the kitchen god, *Zao Jun,* the domestic religion of the Chinese is the province of women. But it is the kitchen god who is believed to confer wealth, civilization, protection, and to assure the cohesion of the social group: all qualities peculiar to men. The ancestral cults are divided into two categories: those celebrated at the shrines of ancestors, and those celebrated in the temples and before the urns. Officiants in the first type of service, who appear before the tablets where their ancestors' names are inscribed, are exposed to the evil influence of the spirits of the dead. And, except in certain élite Confucian circles, it is women who are thought to be able to contact this evil power, take it upon themselves, and exorcise it: the punitive power of the ancestors is passed on through the women.

The situation in the temples and cemeteries is altogether different. This is the men's domain; here, the ancestors are not dead individuals who possess evil powers, but rather they form a 'collective ancestry', the common spiritual property of the economic group. These tombs are the principal site of the agnatic community, in which women have no place; the only way they may enter is as names inscribed on tablets. Woman's domain — the house, the shrines — is a realm of personal relationships between dead and living, a field where evil power — envy, violence, punishment — is exerted. The civilized and civilizing portion, the realm of discipline and cohesion, even within the domestic cult itself, is reserved for the men. In a system where the kitchen is considered a fundamental structure of the social/cultural order, it is the men who pay homage to the kitchen god.[1]

Woman in the symbolic feudal system will represent that aspect of the bipolar structure of family and social order which must be throttled, bridled, marked with the minus sign: she is the negative force, in constant dialogue with death and evil. It is thus that we may interpret that other feudal custom, the crippling of the woman's feet.

The custom seems to date back to the beginning of the tenth century, between the end of the Tang Dynasty (906) and the beginning of the Song (960). It is attributed to one of the great love poets and the second ruler of the Tang Dynasty, Li Yu (937-978), who is supposed to have compelled his favourite Yaoniang to bind her feet so as to dance on the image of a large lotus flower. At first the privilege of the aristocracy, the custom spread throughout the whole population. Mothers perform the operation on their daughters before the little girls' fifth birthdays. The toes are bent under the sole of the foot, and the broken foot is then bound with several metres of bandages that stop the circulation. The operation lasts ten to fifteen years, and the only reward of this unimaginable suffering is that it transforms a woman into a fetish, and, thus, a

---

[1] Cf. Maurice Freedman, 'Ritual Aspect of Chinese Kinship and Marriage', in M. Freedman, ed. *Family and Kinship in Chinese Society*, Stanford, 1970.

pure object of love. By imitating in some way the fate of her mangled and fetishized feet, a woman enters into the 'code of love' — a code of tears and suffering. Outside this code, there is the neutral and non-individual state of peace, of collective and contractual marriage; or there is the well-known eroticism of the peasant, the taoist, or the aristocrat.[1]

The bound foot (euphemistically known as the 'golden lily' or the 'perfumed lily') along with its little staggering dancelike walk — thought to be so erotic — enters courtly literature and sets off waves of adoration among the poets. It becomes the most erotic organ of the female body: Tang painters depict a woman's genitals, but never a naked crippled foot. In addition, a special stocking, whose style changes according to fashion, must cover the foot, even during sexual intercourse, if servants or other witnesses are present. It is not at all shocking that women of many classes rush to submit themselves to the torture: after so many years of suffering, it presents a unique opportunity to gain the respect and recognition of the in-laws, who will praise the beautiful tiny feet even beyond her dowry, as an undeniable proof of her capacity to suffer and obey. The Manchurian Emperor Kangxi was opposed to foot-binding, but, unable to put an end to the practice, he was forced to postpone outlawing it for several years. The custom begins declining after the bourgeois revolution, but it continues to be practised in some areas until the Liberation, despite the injury that it does, not only to women themselves, but to the work force as a whole, where the part they can play is necessarily limited.

A final and not insignificant consequence is that foot-binding impeded the development of dance in China. On the stage of the Peking Opera even today one can see these lithe feminine bodies, with slender torsoes and graceful arms, but with heavy pelvises and stereotyped monotonous steps, where one can read not only the immemorial history of their peasant grandmothers, but probably also this immobility imposed on them for ten centuries by the bound foot. Jiang Qing (Chiang Ching), Mao's

---

[1]Robert Van Gulik, *La vie sexuelle dans la Chine ancienne*, Gallimard, 1972.

present wife, wanted to get rid of all that by introducing 'toe shoes', using sharp instruments, our interpreter He Kejin tells us, that made the feet of Xi'an dancers bleed. If they succeeded in tearing the dancer's hesitant legs away from their fearful contact with the earth, they were as incongruous with their rounded bodies as Swan Lake would be in the plateaux of Tibet. Still a weight of tradition to be lifted; but otherwise than in the Russian manner.

Freud saw in the custom of foot-binding the symbol of the castration of woman which Chinese civilization was unique in admitting. If by 'castration' we understand the necessity for something to be excluded so that a socio-symbolic order may be built — the cutting off of one part of the whole, so that the whole as such may be constituted as an alliance of homogeneous parts — it is interesting to note that for Chinese feudal civilization this 'superfluous' quantity was found in women. Is it simply a matter of knowing that woman does not have a penis? But then the insistence on underlining what's 'missing' in woman by additional symbols (crippling the foot) would tend to prove that they're not all that certain; that some doubt still persists. Does feudal patriarchal society suspect that woman possesses — if not a penile power — a social and symbolic power that remains with her from the early matrilineal tradition? To eliminate this suspicion is thus one aspect of the effort of feudal society to abolish the vestiges of matrilinear descent (bilateral restricted exchange). Wife-sacrificing during the interregnum between the two family models may have been a more savage form of protest against matrilinear descent and against the rights it conferred on the maternal clan. Or, by the implacable logic of symbolism, from the moment when she is branded 'less' (if only to ward off the threat she represents — evil power, matrilinear right), woman is introduced into the phallic order; but as its waste product, its depreciation — a fetish, equivalent to currency, or to any other means of exchange (economic, aesthetic, psychological). Man will not have to assume any part of the loss to which each of the groups that constitute a community must generally assent in order to build the social order: woman will take it entirely upon herself. She will derive suffering and masochistic pleasure from it; but in the long run, she will have the symbolic premium as well: a sort of superior knowledge, a superior maturity, because it is in her feminine world that the difficulty of the social contract is felt, in all its most painful, impossible, murderous aspects. Thus, the depreciation of woman becomes its own opposite: the refuse of society retains society's secret. And if, by some coincidence of circumstance (the right of the eldest daughter, family wealth, etc.) she happens to rise above her condition of silent slavery — the ultimate support of the society so long as she says nothing about it — and gain some access to political and ideological expression, the words and the acts of the Chinese women are striking in their maturity and their historical — if not revolutionary — clair-voyance. Such is obviously not the case for the majority of women, in city and countryside, who have been reduced for-ever to mute objects or slaves to the patriarchal order by foot-binding and all the other practices of family oppression (not least among them being submission to the mother-in-law). But, even in these cases, one wonders if a kind of maturity, a kind of intelligence, a calm, precise mastery does not continue to characterize the Chinese woman and distinguish her from the man — even if such traits remain unrealized in the socio-political sphere. As if the first archaic matriarchal model had avenged itself on the patriarchy by slipping in under the door and drawing certain advantages from the very oppression itself. But we mustn't leave the false impression that, in this frame-work, the man, who apparently holds the power, doesn't suspect its hidden feminine face: we must say first of all that these men are the sons of such mothers; and we have already emphasized the exclusive and passionate relationships of mothers (transients, foreigners) and their sons. Finally, the Taoist tradition has never ceased to fight the Confucian pater-nal hierarchy, so that an ambivalence in paternal/maternal, masculine/feminine roles persists despite everything, on both sides of the sexual border which itself is nevertheless drawn without ambiguity. In any case, one can perceive here all that distinguishes such a system from the monotheistic system: our Western analogue for footbinding is circumcision. So here it is the male rather than the female, who assumes the social and symbolic prohibition, along with the superior political and symbolic knowledge which they confer. In our universe, then, the man takes upon himself both the social prohibition and the symbolic prohibition, with the super-political and super-symbolic knowledge this latter confers: as we suggested above, he is 'his father's daughter'. Whereas in ancient China, a certain balance seems to be reached between the two sexes, although it is shrouded in the great majority of cases by the economic oppression of the women.

I can still see them, in Peking or in the provinces, these elderly women all dressed in black, with tiny babies' feet that I hardly dared to look at, let alone photograph. It doesn't help to know that this tiny foot exists, and that it's very tiny: it is perfectly unimaginable. The miniature black velvet shoes with their cardboard soles are hardly unrealistic: how could these women possibly walk very much? How can they balance the weight of their little dry or rounded bodies? I didn't dare ask them; and those who allude to the bound foot do so only in reference to its impeding their factory work, or to the early retirement the popular government has consequently accorded them. Only the moist, solitary eyes, a bit sad, made for looking inside rather than directly at you — only the eyes, with their soft, veiled irony, betray these women's suffering. In the evening, their sons and grandsons carry them on the backs of their bicycles like wounded Amazons. On the eve of May Day in Peking, when the lanterns are lit and everyone pours into the forbidden ancient city, Tiananmen Square is full of Red Guards on their bicycles, ferrying their crippled grandmothers through the crowd.

In the vast army of the anonymous, some few have managed to make and leave a name for themselves: concubines, courtesans, a few empresses, a woman poet, a few women soldiers, and a few victims of the national cause.

There is even one who is more Confucian than the Confucians: Pan Zhao (d. A.D. 116). The daughter and sister of famous *literati*, she was widowed at an early age and devoted herself entirely to her writing. The most notable of her works is the *Nüjie*, 'The Precepts for Women', which exalts the submission and self-effacement of women before the authority of father or husband. We quote:

> In truth, as far as knowledge goes, a woman need not be
> extraordinarily intelligent. As for her speech, it need not
> be terribly clever. As for her appearance, it need not be
> beautiful or elegant; and as for her talents, they need
> only be average. . . . This is why the *Nüxian* says 'If a
> wife is like a shadow or an echo, how can you fail to
> praise her?'

The concubines: Ordinary concubines are anonymous. The
few who are famous come from the ranks of the court,
gracious women expert in love, and intelligent women who
govern the Empire through the Emperor, for better or for
worse. Two famous examples, among many others:

Chen Yuanyuan, the mistress of General Wu Sangui, is
captured by enemies. The General enters the Capitol for the
sole purpose of liberating her, but his act has historical consequences: the foundation of the Manchurian Dynasty, to
which the General surrenders himself.

Another concubine, Li Xiangjun, falls into captivity while
the enemies of her lord are invading Nanking. She decides to
protest by fasting until she can rejoin him. The enemies,
worried by Li Xiangjun's fame, don't want to appear to be
making her suffer, and force her to sing at a banquet. But
there, the courageous concubine neither bursts into tears nor
remains silent; instead, she improvises song after song,
satirizing her jailers. Impressed by her independence, they free
her.

Others excel in the art of war. Liang Hongyu, originally a
prostitute, becomes the concubine of General Han Shizhong
under the Song, and learns the strategy of war merely as a
means of relieving her boredom in the house. But war breaks
out against 'the barbarians', the games of war turn serious,
and Liang Hongyu valiantly leads the troops in the front line
of battle.

Finally, certain concubines, like Yang Guifei, distinguish
themselves by their participation in cultural affairs. Legend or
history attributes to them the initiative in building roads or
protecting great works of art. On the other hand, the defeat of

the State of the Emperor Ming Huang (745) is attributed to this same famous beauty, Yang Guifei, his concubine-turned-imperial bride, and to her brother, his minister. A rebellion among the soldiers demanded that the Emperor strangle Yang Guifei in exchange for the continued defence of the state against enemy troops. One of the palaces built for Yang Guifei still stands today at the thermal baths near Xi'an; visitors still come to see the perfumed halls and the marble pool, in the shape of three linked ellipses, where this concubine, whose politics and imagination are fouled by history, bathed her mute and graceful body.

Only one of these famous concubines succeeded in freeing herself from her role as servant — however intrepid and intelligent — to become the Empress. Originally the wife of the Emperor Taizong, later the favourite of his son Gaozong, Wu Zhao (642-703) gets rid of the Empress and another favourite of the Emperor by accusing them of the murder of her child — whom in fact she has killed herself. She is proclaimed Empress in 655. After the death of Gaozong, in 690, she assumes the title of *Emperor* and the name Wu Zetian. Wu Zetian rules the Empire with a firm hand, and is still famous for her independent life-style (probably exaggerated by the Confucian historians whose opinions she neglected in favour of those of the Buddhist clergy), but also for her consolidation of Imperial power. Wu Zetian undercuts the influence of the ruling class (the rich families); she institutes the system of competitive examinations for civil servants, who did not play a very great role under the Han, but who would become the pillar of the Chinese political system; she transforms the administrative structure, creates new guidelines for personal surnames, changes the names of geographic places, and even invents nineteen new written characters. A former Buddhist nun, Wu Zetian anchored her power in Buddhist authority; but she gave a great deal to the Buddhist Church in exchange. Not far from the city of Luoyang, one can still visit the famous Longmen caves that the Buddhists began to excavate during her reign. In Confucian China, Buddhism (like Taoism, and, later, Christianity) was frequently the refuge of women, since, unlike Confucianism, it acknowledged — at least theoretically — their equality with men.

Before Wu Zetian, one Queen had been remembered as the defender of the people: Queen Wei, widow of Zhao, receives the messenger of the King Jian of Qi (264-221 B.C.) and asks him, 'Has the year been good? Do the people prosper?' And only last, 'Is the King in good health?' 'How can you give first place to what is base and vile, and last to what is noble and venerable?' says the messenger, astonished. And Wei answers him, 'If there were no harvest, how could there be a people? And if there were no people, how could there be a King? So then, is it required to ask about the less important, and leave the more important aside?'[1]

The end of the Qing Empire sees the reign of the famous Empress Xiaoqin (Cixi-Tz'u-hsi), who dominates the political life of China from 1875 until her death in 1908. It is a troubled time: weakened by the Taiping Revolt, the country is facing the penetration of capitalist economy and, at the same time, the war waged by foreign colonialists. Partisans of the new economic system are violently opposed by more traditional thinkers; the pillaging of Japanese, Russian, French, and English colonizers continues; local powers seize increasing control from the central government, and 'modernization' fails. During this period the court is cut off from the real socio-economic problems, and Cixi uses her imagination and all her shrewd intelligence to keep herself in power, steering a narrow course between 'modernists' and 'conservatives'. This Empress, who ferociously undercuts several attempts at reform, and cruelly persecutes her son Guangxu, did not, however, lack a certain charm, even in the eyes of her most rebellious subjects. The proof of it is this statement by Mao, doubtless tongue-in-cheek, where he compares her to Stalin: both are referred to as Lao Zuzong, 'old ancestor', both stirring in him a mixture of disgust and respect.

> So that our comrades may recognize that the 'old ancestor' also has her faults, one must analyze the

---

[1]Cf. *Le Kouwen Chinois*, collection of texts with introduction and notes by G. Margolies, Paris, P. Geuthner, 1926.

phenomenon and not just blindly believe in it.[1]

One finds mention of the *courtesans* from the time of the Zhou Dynasty (1st millenium B.C.) on wards. They seem originally to have been an accepted institution of patriarchal society: an outlet for the energy that ritual and celebration were not enough to satisfy, and where men and women, without guilt or debasement, could act out a desire that the new patriarchal family structure failed to inhibit. Later, under the Han, the Tang, and even the Song, female prostitution, while considered 'outside' the acceptable social/familial order, was not regarded with the same contempt as in the Christian West: many daughters of wealthy families turned more or less openly to it, not to speak of the covert prostitution that went on in Buddhist and Taoist monasteries, where widows and wealthy ladies — but also local peasant women — sought refuge from Confucian moralism without having to publicly acknowledge their trade. From the time of the Mongolian Empire of the Yuan (13th-14th century), under which the mass return of the Chinese to Confucianism seems to have been a means of protection against the invader — and especially under the Ming (1368-1644), who reinforced the neo-Confucianism of the Song and began persecuting Buddhists and Taoists accused of engaging in sexual acts which did not lead to procreation — prostitution became a forbidden profession. For that very reason it was all the more necessary and more in demand: a vice useful to the law, a transgression that inspired the moral code and allowed it to exist. Marco Polo says he found approximately 20,000 prostitutes in the suburbs of Peking. In more recent times, colonialism — with its opium — widely exploited this base: the coincidences of the old feudal morality and western mores has, in the eyes of the modern Chinese, turned prostitution — and with it, all commercialized and even extramarital sex — into a curse of the old regime. The problem of finding a channel for sexual energy in a socialist society through various forms of sublimation outside the family

---

[1] "Discussion at the Chengdu Conference," March 1958, in *Mao Tse-tung Unrehearsed, talks and letters: 1956-71*, edited by Stuart Schram, Penguin Books, 1974, pp. 101, 307.

(political, aesthetic, etc.) has not as yet been dealt with officially in China. If the question should be asked one day, and if the analysis of Chinese tradition that the *Pi Lin Pi Kong Campaign* seems to have undertaken is not interrupted, it's not altogether impossible that China may approach it with much less prudishness and fetishist neurosis than the Christian West has managed while clamouring for 'sexual freedom'.

Female literati, even among the leisure classes, are rare at the beginning of the Empire: we hear of the strange case of Su Hui (around A.D. 350), the wife of a prefect under the Jin. Jealous of her husband's concubine, she beats her, and does not redeem herself in her husband's eyes until she has embroidered a love poem of 841 characters! Under the Tang (618-906), courtesan/*literati* are more numerous; but only two left any original work: Yu Xuanji (844-871) and Xue Dao (786-831). Under the Song (960-1279) education for women begins to be more common, and they learn not only to write, but also — for the first time — to paint. Two names are remembered from this period: Lady Xu, the wife of a famous general, who left a rich collection of 'palace songs' under the pseudonym 'Lady Flower Stamen' (*c.* 935), and Lady Guan Daochen (1262-1319), who wrote love poems about the psychology of the couple, and did fine bamboo paintings. But the name of one woman — still of the Song Dynasty — dominates Chinese literature: Li Qingzhao.

Classical authors as well as modern critics (Guo Muoro among them) agree in placing her among the greatest Chinese writers, beside Li Bai, Du Fu, etc.; certainly she is the finest of the Chinese women writers, though she is not categorized simply as such. Li Qingzhao's social origins are naturally favourable to her talent: born in 1081 to a family of *literati*, her father's father was a civil servant and her mother — herself an educated woman — was the daughter of the first mandarin of the period. Li Qingzhao married an intellectual, a man who was first a student at the Imperial University and later a great bibliophile and collector of antiques. She became his active collaborator. The work of this remarkable woman poet — perhaps among the greatest, not only in China, but in the literature of the entire world — falls into two categories, which correspond to two periods of her life. The first is written in the *Ci* genre: song-poems in verse considered irregular by comparison to classical quatrains, and closer to folklore and musical rhythms than poetry structured along Confucian lines. The cycle essentially evokes a natural/psychological state of drunkenness, melancholy: subtle sexual allusions, tears, abandon, hope of meeting the beloved, moon, return of spring. Hers are all classical themes of Chinese poetry, where no internal psychological state is presented without a correlative in the natural world, and where the movements of the body and the language itself are intimately woven with the cycles of nature. Li Qingzhao breathes into these universal traits of Chinese poetry a musicality rarely attained by other poets:[1] the brilliantly intertwined rhythms and alliterations, the shape of the characters themselves, create a language where the least aural or visual element becomes the bearer of this symbiosis between body, world, and sense, a language that one cannot label 'music' or 'meaning' because it is both at once.

> xun xun mi mi
> (to look to look to grope to grope)
> leng leng qing qing
> (cold cold green [limped, solitude] green)
> qi qi can can qi qi
> (sad sad pitiful pitiful confusion confusion)
>
> wu tong gen jian xi yu
> (and the plane tree collecting fine rain)
> dao huang hun dian dian di di
> (until the dark yellow [twilight] drop drop droplet droplet)
> zhe ci di
> (this time)
> zen yi ge chou zi liao de
> (how a single word sadness is enough)

Here is a translation (from a French version by Philippe Sollers):

---

[1]On Li Qingzhao, cf. Chantal Andro-Chen, *Les Poémes de Li Qingzhao*, 1081-1141, 3rd form thesis, University of Paris VIII.

here here there there
cold cutting green ice
nothing nothing fear fear
plane tree in fine rain
yellow day darkening drop by drop
this time one
word death won't be enough

When the Golden Horde invades the Song capitol, Bian-liang (now Kaifeng in Henan), Li Qingzhao flees south with her husband. Their papers are burned, their money lost. Her husband finally dies, and she begins the difficult life of an ailing widow fleeing her enemies. It is thus that Li Qingzhao changes her style and begins to write classical poems on national themes, on the wretchedness of the invaded country, on patriotic death, with strong allusions to the abuse of imperial power as the cause of national disaster. A dark period in her life in which she will be faced with the fate of all independent intellectual women, not only those under feudal regimes: she is blamed for remarrying, and even accused of treason, which the historical facts do not seem to justify. Nonetheless, she remains a strong writer, increasingly out-spoken on political themes, increasingly serious about social concerns (she who had involved herself in politics only to defend the merits of her father, stripped of his office, now concerns herself with the fate of the nation). An extremely cultured woman, who does not hesitate to pass severe judgment on poets who have preceded her, or on her contemporaries.[1]

Let us quote two short verses by Li Qingzhao, extracted from larger works: [Tr: These are translated from versions by Liang Paitchin, who has translated an entire collection of her work.]

Don't underestimate the opinions of the literati
Victory was announced in writing beside a saddled horse

(allusion to the intellectual Yuan, who stood beside his horse

---

[1] Cf. her essay, 'Remarks on the Song Poem', where she accuses the majority of poets of failing to make their poems musical enough.

and read his victory poem before leaving for battle), or:

> Success and failure are decided:
> The first and the last are marked.
> All orders begin in the little square inch of our mind.
> Who can say what the end of the battle
> Will be? Our horses are in the field.

> The desire to triumph
> Is an instinct of man,
> The art of enjoyment
> A refined game of the literati.
> (from 'The Game of the Little Horses')

An identification with men, an insistence on the values of the *literati*, a fascination with power and success: So be it. But there is also in Li Qingzhao a reminder of the political power of the (astonishingly accurate) written word, a defence of personal initiative against all orders. And all this in a musical, precise, and economical language that no translation can hope to reproduce. Li Qingzhao is the perfect example of the kind of excellence a woman can achieve on the condition that she cease to live as a woman.

One prototype that has served as a model for many Chinese girls and women who have wished to abandon a strictly feminine role and gain access to the political sphere is Hua Mulan, the heroine of the Five Dynasties (420-588). A legendary figure, she has remained famous because of an anonymous poet who sang her praises in the famous 'Song of Mulan'. So much does she love her father that, when he is called to battle against the Tartars and finds himself unable to go, she goes in his place, disguised as a man. For twelve years Hua Mulan serves as a transvestite in the army, without anyone suspecting her. Once victory is won, she puts back on her make-up and her women's clothes: a quick-change act, a permanent masquerade (as a man *and* as a woman) that spares this Chinese Clorinda the tragedy of ours. This story repeats itself, in legend and reality, throughout the years of China's past; but we find it even today in the manuals of young Chinese describing the war against Japan.

Finally, another frequent theme is that of the 'worthy' Chinese woman, she who braves death by letting herself be killed without inching before the enemy, or by committing suicide to facilitate the patriotic or revolutionary task of her husband or her clan. The *Guwen*, a collection of classical texts, includes a request that has become famous as an example of a wife's willingness to sacrifice herself in order to save her husband. Yang Jisheng (1516-1556), an intellectual and politician, was unjustly accused and threatened with death. His wife writes:

> 'If, unworthy insect that I am, (the Emperor) sees fit to grant me his favour and make the punishment a bit less severe, my happiness will know no bounds. If it is too serious a crime for him to pardon, I myself would like to be brought immediately to the market place of the capital, and have my head cut off in place of my husband's.'

Her husband was beheaded nevertheless, though his reputation was cleared by the successor of the unjust Emperor.[1]

In numerous stories, it is a woman soldier and not a man who prefers to be tortured by the enemy rather than reveal the names of her comrades: as if the authors of these tales or reports were fascinated by the detachment of women going to their deaths without tragedy, without seeming to be giving up anything too precious; but as though they were performing a perfectly natural act which would bring them not only popular glory, but some special secret pleasure as well. I was surprised to discover that a Chinese friend who, in her youth, fought alongside the Chinese feminists, and who today writes literary texts about the great deeds of Chinese women, could find no better examples to illustrate her defence and her portrait of women in China than the stories of women who committed suicide: a concubine who drives a sword into her breast to avoid committing adultery and get her lord/emperor out of some political jam; a communist who kills herself in prison to prevent the capture of a comrade who, one is led to

---

[1]Cf. *Le Kouwen Chinois*, collection of texts with introduction and notes by G. Margoulies, Paris, P. Geuthner, 1926.

believe, may be none other than Mao. . . .

Concubines who lead the Empire to its fall or its flowering, in the shadows of their lords. Women who put on men's battle-dress to replace their fathers or serve the cause. Martyrdom, sacrifice, suicide: there is the inventory of political functions a woman may perform. There were exceptions in more than two thousand years: one woman Emperor (Wu Zetian), thanks to circumstances and the clergy; and one poet (Li Qingzhao), thanks to talent and family. Beginning with the last decade of the nineteenth century, the Chinese woman will have to triumph over the family, as well as the world of politics: and not for a minute can she have the one victory without the other.

*　　*　　*

It is impossible to measure the influence that this Confucian conception of women and family had on Chinese mores. There are strong chances for its survival after so many years of practice, and it will take more to wipe it out than an anti-Confucian campaign which is itself stained with unconscious vestiges of the old days. Let us examine the findings of a few researchers on family psychology or its representation in modern fiction, as a means of understanding the forms these feudal/Confucian mores take in Chinese culture today.

We can develop some idea of what the inter-familial relationship in pre-liberation continental China were like from the results of a study of a village in Taiwan where traditional family relationships are thought to persist. Until a son reaches the age of six or seven, his relationship with his father is close and affectionate: the son sleeps on his father's lap, wanders about with him, snuggles up to his father's body as he would to his mother's. Afterward, there is a brutal change: distance on the father's part and filial piety on the son's are demanded but the father's punishments are less severe than the mother's, which are violent and emotional, and often arise from the frustrations of the day. The relationship between mother and son is coloured by the fact that the son is the chief means by which the 'stranger' achieves recognition in the new family. In addition, the son is aware that he will ultimately be dependent on his mother, who will be considered superior to his wife and

95

will be the final authority on the education of his children. Although the complexities of this relationship are not explicitly expressed, they determine to a great degree the furious nature of the arguments between mother and son, and are responsible for a sort of unspoken passion between them. Altogether different is the relationship between father and daughter, which is not accounted for in the human relationships outlined by Confucius. Here, obedience does not exclude intimacy, nor even a certain disrespect, when that does not denote a cynical element in their dealings with one another. It is rather to her mother that a girl owes perfect obedience: she is subject to the mother's authority even after she marries and leaves the family home, at which point her father's authority is replaced by that of her husband, but her mother's remains the same. It is interesting to note that this situation of the daughter with regard to the two parents induces a precocious socialization in her, which comes across — in the various tests administered by the researchers — in performances that are far superior to those of boys the same age. In her new family, the daughter-in-law fears above all the authority of her mother-in-law, with whom she wages a desperate battle for the affection of her husband and the education of her children. In this, the daughter-in-law is helped by the ambivalence in the relationship between her father-in-law and her husband. If filial piety is due to the elderly father, it seems that his power does not go uncontested, and that the elderly mother definitely makes herself heard through her son; even if, when she dies, she is entitled to far less extravagant funeral rites than her husband. This portrait[1] pinpoints quite well the various modes of anxiety and self-defence of women in an androcentric society, where they actualize themselves only as the cherished daughters of their fathers or as ageing mothers lording it over their sons, exhausting their strength in a continuous war of the passions with other women (mother, daughter, mother-in-law), a war of whose issues and strategies little is known, but whose

---

[1]Traced by Margery Wolf, 'Child Training and the Chinese Family', in M. Freedman, ed., *Family and Kinship in Chinese Society,* Stanford University Press, 1970.

sexual and symbolic overtones can well be imagined.

The literature of the 'thirties and 'forties provides us with an even more lucid portrait of the Confucian family under the pressure of the new capitalism that began to penetrate China toward the end of the nineteenth century, bringing with it the various socialist, anarchist, or libertarian ideologies which eventually led to the bourgeois revolution of 1912 and the 4th of May movement of 1919. This crisis of the Chinese family and of patriarchal morality shattered the contractual peace of the *jia* with a passion whose tragic force has suggested comparison with early Greek drama. In fact, in the work of the celebrated playwright Cao Yu, the fruitless, aggressive attack on paternal authority results in incest between mother and son (cf. *The Storm*). Or it is the intrusion of the stranger which explodes the strained civility of the Confucian family by revealing to it the repressed desire which ultimately destroys it (cf. *The Man from Peking*). In a more clearly anarchist view, the trilogy of Ba Jin — *Family, Spring, Autumn* — depicts the revolt of the sons against the fathers which is the constant motif of the literature of May 4, as well as that of the 'thirties.

An interesting study of the representation of family relationships in modern fiction and, notably, in the short stories published by the Taiwan review, *Xiandai Wenxue*, throws some light on the subsequent evolution of the Confucian family in a bourgeois regime, and, therefore, without the socialist revolution. Out of forty-nine stories published in this magazine before 1960, 59% are about family relationships, while the rest depict isolated individuals and their ill-fated sexual encounters. Twenty-two stories are about the mother/son relationship — twice as many as those dealing with fathers and sons and three times the number of stories about father/daughter or mother/daughter relationships. A certain decline in the father's prestige is evident beside the traditional Confucian portrait of him as distant and withdrawn: he does not always possess the experience or the intelligence required by modern circumstances, even if he still takes the option of beating his son. The mother is possessive, and echoes the harsh attitude of her husband; she is bitter toward her children, whom she accuses of having ruined her life. The girl remains a rebel: she disobeys her father, and frequently displays a deeply negative attitude toward her mother. It is curious to note that the so-called 'modern relationships' between boys and girls of these post-Confucian families are characterized in these stories by mutual suspicion and fear of being ridiculed, deceived, or betrayed. Those stories that deal with married couples, far from reviving the themes dear to the spirit of emancipation that marked the famous bourgeois movement of 4 May 1919, present the husband/wife relationship as an unending struggle for dominance, waged with a mutual lack of sensitivity, sympathy, and understanding.[1] Individualism and bourgeois psychology don't seem to be able to grow in Confucian soil except in their most wretched varieties: destroying the old family harmony (however damaging that may have been), they replace it with neither the jovial cynicism of the bourgeois renaissance nor the pleasant fetishism of the 'belle époque', but rather with a bitter indictment of the patriarchal family and the society (feudal or bourgeois) from which it arises.

Whether as a result of the vestiges of the first (matrilinear) family model, of the subtle presence of Taoism, or of the internal complexity of Confucianism itself, hierarchial paternal/paternalistic ritualism is clearly and constantly accompanied by customs and practices that allow the yin to slip through. The yin, this feminine which is not necessarily 'a woman' and which, in the structure of a custom, is the reverse, the opposite of dominance, the empty, the timeless. To me, there is no better evidence of its persistence — through the accidents of history and up to the present — than the fluid precision of 'Chinese gymnastics', Taiji quan (Tai Chi). Early in the morning or at twilight, on the banks of the Huangbu or at the edge of a street swarming with pedestrians, bodies launch themselves into a lover's dance with space. The initial thrust propels the body into a series of movements where figures follow one after another in an involuntary rhythm. Neither conscious nor automatic, neither slack nor abrupt: squares become circles and circles become squares, as though the body were appro-

---

[1] Cf. Ai-Li S. Chin ,'Family Relations in Modern Chinese Fiction,' in M. Freedman, *op. cit.*, 1970.

priating the surrounding void in order to bring it inside, and to give the outside fullness and dimension. There is no tension in the muscle, nor weight to the bone: the rhythm of this game, where the partner is space, seems to flow with the blood. It is true that Tai Chi has been traditionally reserved for men. But in modern times, and especially today, women — from grandmothers to little girls — excel in this art which emphasizes the difference (*always* and *simultaneously* sexual, rhythmic, spatial and temporal) in each individual body. Beyond and beside Confucianism, there unfolds another scene, where a single individual — man or woman — is constantly changing with respect to the void: a new 'amorous body', that mimes the erotic dance with 'the other' by ceaseless differentiation — inside/outside, time/timelessness. . . . Beside it, on the surface, ideology may reign: Confucian, ritualist, oppressive, dogmatic. But ever surpassed by this rhythm, of which Tai Chi is but one of the forms.

III

Socialism and Feminism

In the Chinese bourgeois revolution of the beginning of the century, elements of national liberation (to overthrow Manchurian feudalism), socialist ideology (the bourgeois West, which inspired the revolt, already dreamed of a new society, and the Paris Commune had already fought for it), and the emancipation of women (because to combat feudalism is first of all to combat the Confucian family and morality) were indissolubly linked. These currents may be traced in each particular and collective action of Chinese women of that period.

The first woman militants in the bourgeois-nationalist-socialist revolution are, naturally, daughters of the leisure class who have been educated in Japan or in Europe. Helen Foster Snow has recently discussed the role played by Christian (particularly Protestant) women in the propagation of a spirit of autonomy and liberation among young Chinese girls.[1] This influence is indisputable among the educated daughters of the élite, and is confirmed in the biographies of the famous women of the Chinese bourgeois revolution who surrounded Sun Yixian (Sun Yatsen) and were in the Guomindang. But we must insist on the fact that, in Chinese high society, and particularly in non-Han, non-Confucian families, a certain freedom was accorded to women — ambiguous but nonetheless

---

[1]Cf. Helen Foster Snow, *Women in Modern China*, Mouton, 1967.

effective. Thus, the daughters of Taoist 'Boxers' received a military education like their brothers, and took part in political struggles as rebels or 'bandits' fighting against feudal law. In the nineteenth century, the Taiping rebellion, which inherited this tradition and Christianized it, was carried out by separate units of men and women, each with its own command. The female brigades of the Taiping were supposed to perform traditionally 'feminine' jobs — weaving, etc. — but they were also instructed in the art of war. During the first phase of the bourgeois nationalist revolution, before 1911, women participated essentially as teachers, journalists, or students spreading the new ideas; but they also joined forces in the *National Women's Army*, the *Corps of Women Who Dare To Die*, that is, the Women's Volunteer Corps, and the Women's Assassination Corps, all of which actively helped the men's troops in their efforts from the end of the nineteenth century onwards. A famous example from this period was Sophia Chang, who took the name of a Russian woman, Sophia Pirovskaia, who had participated in attempts to assassinate Alexander II.

After the foundation of the republic, the women's brigades were considered to be too dangerous, and were disbanded by the provisional government of Nanking. At this point, the non-military wing of the *Women's Rights Movement* came into action. One woman of the pre-Republican period is particularly memorable: Qiu Jin. Born in 1874, the daughter of wealthy intellectuals, educated in Japan, unhappy with her arranged marriage, she leaves her husband and her two children to devote herself to national liberation. Influenced as well by Russian anarchists, she founds a school for girls, teaches in a school for boys, and starts the first women's newspaper in China. Dressed as a man and riding the streets on horseback, this intellectual militant inspires fascination, indignation, and admiration in those who see her. Along with her cousin, she plots an armed uprising in the region of Jiangxi against the Qing monarchy, and attempts to assassinate the governor. Arrested, convicted, she refuses to make a confession; and, before her execution in 1907, without letting a single word pass her lips, she writes these austere anonymous poems where an anagram of her name can be found:

101

Qiu feng qi yu/chou sha ren
The autumn wind and the autumn rain
Make us think sadly of death

Beside Qiu Jin's name, on a posthumously published collection
of her poems, Sun Yatsen has affixed the title, 'Heroine Among
Women'. In one of these poems, 'Fight for the Power of
Women', we read:

May Heaven grant equal power to men and women
Is it pleasant to live lower than cattle?
We will raise ourselves to the sky, yes,
Our bodies will soar in flight

Qiu Jin's daughter was educated in the United States, and
became the first woman aviator in China.

The true Chinese feminist movement begins at the very
start of the bourgeois Republic founded in 1912. Deeply
influenced by western suffragettes, but coloured as well by the
fight against a feudal patriarchal society, this movement calls
itself 'nüguan yundong', — 'women's rights movement' — or
'canzheng yundong', 'suffrage movement'. Its goal is to support
the Republic and to work for equal rights for men and women.
The movement combines the efforts of several organizations,
among them the *Shanghai Social Club for Women's Suffrage*,
the *Militant Women's Society*, the *Female Alliance*, the
Women's Organization for Peace, and the *Women's Citizens
Society*.[1] These organizations meet on 22 January 1912 to
form a co-ordinating council and to make public a list of
the objectives that will later be adopted by the 4 May 1919
movement. Among these objectives are: equal rights for men
and women, higher education for women, abolition of polygamy and the selling of women, freedom of choice in marriage,
reformation of family customs. As Roxane Witke says (*op. cit.*),
these demands proved that, as far back as 1912, the Chinese
political revolution had out-distanced the social revolution.

---

[1]Cf. Roxane Witke, 'Woman as Politician in China of the 1920's,'
in *Women in China*, edited by Marilyn B. Young, Michigan Papers
in Chinese Studies, 1973.

The role of the women's movement was to work for sweeping social reform; and this work, which may have appeared out of phase with the actual political scene, was no less dedicated to the truly universal transformation of Chinese society. However, the unequal rates of political and social development created tremendous difficulties for the women's struggle, by confronting it with this ultimatum: either the women's movement would continue as such, but more or less outside the main political arena, or the movement could integrate itself with these political parties and events, but at the cost of its own specificity.

In May, 1912, this problem comes abruptly to the surface. A provisional constitution is approved (11 May) without a single mention of sexual equality. One week later (20 May) a group of women submit a petition to Sun Yatsen. Promises are made, nothing is done. The anger erupts. Some feminists and their supporters storm Parliament, smashing windows and injuring several guards. The eyes of China — and of the West as well — open wide in astonishment: no one would have expected this of Oriental suffragettes. Now their rage has made them exist in the eyes of the world. Their example is followed throughout the country, and similar petitions are brought before the legislative bodies of several provinces, beginning with Jiangsu.

After the Second Revolution in 1913, and the failure of the republican ideas, the military arena again becomes the important one, and women participate actively. But the nationalist or socialist revolutions are already sensitized to the problems of women and the family: no reform movement will henceforth be possible in China unless it takes them into account. Publications appear, criticizing the impact of Confucianism on the Chinese family,[1] while others attempt to fit the women's movement into a Marxist conception of class struggle: a contradiction or a strategic alliance between Marxism and feminism?[2]

---

[1]Cf. Chen Duxiu, 'Confucianism and modern life', in *Xin Qingnian* (New Youth), December 1916.
[2]Li Dazhao, 'The movement for the rights of modern women', in *Funü pinglun (Feminine Critique)*, n. 25, 28 February 1922.

The Movement of 4 May 1919 adopts these ideas and spreads them throughout the country: The emancipation of women becomes a constant theme of 4 May, but nothing more than a theme: no concrete action follows the propaganda. During this second wave of the Chinese suffragette movement, many women take part in the bourgeois nationalist struggle for provincial autonomy (in Hunan and Guangdong at first); but they take part as well in the International Council of Suffragettes in Switzerland in 1920. The famous 'Five Propositions' of Chinese suffragettes date from this time: equal rights of inheritance, the right to vote and to be elected, equal rights in work and education, the right of self-determination in marriage, and free choice in marriage. Acting principally in urban centres, recruiting among intellectuals and among women factory workers, and frequently counting two male members to every female, the suffragette societies manage to gain some ground. In Hunan, for instance, the right of women to vote and to be elected is immediately recognized and enforced. A similar, but unsuccessful, attempt is made in Peking by women students at the very famous Upper Normal School, who attempt to have the constitution modified to include a clause providing equality not only of race and nationality, but sex as well. Too soon: the issue was still open in France in 1974!

Having first supported the central republican government, and then fought for provincial autonomy, and having actively collaborated in the spirit of emancipation of May 4, the Chinese suffragette movement finds itself henceforth backed into a corner. The majority of active militants persist in their methods of propaganda and education through the press and the schools; but they will find themselves set off from the immediate concerns of the masses first by the political struggles and then by the Japanese invasion. The most radical among them will join the two parties, the Guomindang and the Communist Party, in a more or less successful attempt to reconcile the 'party line' with feminist demands. It is interesting to note that, even today, it is women peasants and intellectuals, rather than factory workers, who continue to be concerned with specifically feminist demands. This may be explained, on the one hand, by the sensitization of intellectuals to the ideological changes in a society where, as products of the leisure class, they do not suffer socio-economic discrimination; as for the peasants, their concern may be attributed to the persistence of patriarchal feudal power in the countryside, where family oppression has not been influenced at all by the ideas of 4 May. On the contrary, the movement of Chinese women labourers would have, from the start, essentially economic demands, which would coincide more or less with the policies of the Chinese Communist Party. The demand for political rights is accompanied in some places by a transformation in mores, itself made possible by the development of a bourgeois economy and, more specifically, by the financial independence that a woman — daughter of a wealthy family or worker in a big city — may attain in such an economy. Thus, female homosexuality, previously hidden in the closets of the polygamous family, manifests itself more directly, if still somewhat secretly, in the formation of secret lesbian societies known as 'zi shu nü' — 'women who do their own hair'. These societies recruit not only among the students of Hunan of bourgeois or aristocratic origin, but among the silk factory workers in Guangdong as well. The gross exportation of silk to America necessitates a very large female labour-force; this makes for a vast army of socially independent women who can thus allow themselves to flee the shelter as well as the oppression of the Confucian family. For the 'women who do their own hair', the husband — who previously has been necessary only as a means of financial support — ceases to be necessary as a sexual partner. A 'resurgence' of the old matriarchy, accompanying the revolt against the fathers? But how was the question of maternity resolved? In an (unlikely) total refusal? Or else as a step taken outside the frame of marriage, or in a temporary marriage? Nothing said by these 'women who do their own hair', nor by outside sociologists, seems to throw very much light on the lives of these communities. Although some few persisted until the war, most of them disbanded during the economic recession of the 'thirties.

One supporter of the suffragettes, Mao Tse-tung, distinguished himself as early as 1919 in a series of articles on 'the condition of women', which come as a surprise to the Western reader. A few biographical facts will help us to understand this position. As he admits to Edgar Snow, Mao suffered greatly when, at the age of thirteen, his father, a middle income Confucian peasant, wanted to marry him to an older woman, as was common in the countryside. Finding no understanding except from his Buddhist mother, the young Mao was frequently in conflict with his father. He tells Snow of an argument in which, when his father forced him to a humiliating display of filial piety, Mao threatened to commit suicide, and finally ran away from home.[1] Later on he would marry Yang Kaihui, whose father, Yang Changji, was Mao's philosophy teacher at the Normal School at Changsha, and was considered a liberal man, an ardent partisan of the ideas of 4 May, and a well-known author. Among other things, Yang wrote a noted article on 'The Reform of The Chinese Family Institution', in which he compares the Chinese family to the English, and suggests the patriarchal family as a major reason for China's weakness. To the probable influence of these ideas on Mao were added not only his reading of the extremely daring magazine *New Youth,* but also the example of the particularly active feminist struggle among the students at Hunan (see above), with whom Mao was in constant contact. It was during this period that he said to his friends, 'I think that the Chinese people are so lacking in nationalist feeling because the Chinese family is so strong.'[2]

In 1917, Mao and his friend Cai Hesheng founded *The Society for the Study of the New People* (Xinmin Xuehui), which proposed to fight prostitution, concubinage, and the abuse of family power; to raise the consciousness of women and help them to discover their social function; and to reform China and the world. Mao himself was considered to be the editor of the founding manifesto. To protest against the old marriage customs the members of the society decided not to

---

[1]Cf. Edgar Snow, *Red Star over China,* New York, Random House 1938.
[2]Cf. Siao Yü, *Mao Tse-tung and I were Beggars,* Syracuse University Press, 1959.

marry; a gesture inspired less by puritanism (especially considering that every member was eventually to go back on his word) than by rebelliousness. Another interesting fact: among the activities of the Society was the creation of a *Programme of Studies in France* (Liufa Qingong Jianxuehui) which sent Chinese youth — and particularly girls — to France. Mao, one of the sponsors of this programme, said to Xiang Jingyu before the group's departure: 'I hope you will be able to lead these women comrades abroad, for each one you take with you is a saved woman.'

We find among the participants in this *Programme of Studies in France* the two women most responsible for the feminist struggles in China during the period that follows: Xiang Jingyu, a student in the Girls' Normal School of Hunan, and Cai Chang, the sister of Cai Hesheng, who was to become the first president of the *Union of Chinese Women* after the Liberation. The members of these societies and programmes became fervent supporters of the ideas of 4 May, and, consequently, belonged to the best-known cadres of the Chinese Communist movement.

But before the foundation of the Chinese Communist Party, and on the heels of the 4th of May Movement, Mao, who was openly concerned with the feminist movement and saw in it a radical means of transforming society, undertook a broad journalistic campaign for women's rights. A study by Roxane Witke[1] discusses Mao's feminist writings between 1919-1920, and specifically those articles which were not published in his *Complete Works*. The earliest among these are articles published in the *Xiang River Review* (Xiangjiang Pinglun), of which Mao was editor-in-chief: in the first issue, Mao signs his article 'The Women's Revolutionary Army'; in issues two, three, and four, Mao points out that women frequently support the old ways of thinking, and calls for them to join the whole human race (of which they are a part — *ren* — and from which Confucius had excluded them by declaring them *xiao ren* — inferior humans) in the struggle against cannibalistic feudal

---

[1] 'Mao Tse-tung, women, and suicide', in *Women in China, op. cit.,* Michigan Papers in Chinese Studies, 1973.

morality: 'Since we are all human beings, why shouldn't we be able to vote? And since we are all human beings, why shouldn't we mix freely together?'

With equal violence, Mao fights against the requirement of chastity, reminding his reader that no one ever demanded that men be chaste. After the magazine was forbidden to publish, Mao published elsewhere. After some time, he became editor-in-chief of the *New Hunan*, where he continued to protest against the 'three bondages' (according to Confucius: to the lord, to the father, to the husband) of women and to fight for their liberation. Finally, he collaborated on the magazine of the Chounan Girls Secondary School, *The Women's Bell* (Nüjie Zhong), whose motto was: 'Goal: liberty and equality; means: struggle, creativity, a women's solution to women's problems.' It is there that Mao seems to have published articles on the suicide of women; but of all he wrote on this subject, only the nine articles published in 1919 in the chief daily paper of Changsha Da Gongbao are currently available.[1] These nine articles are devoted to the suicide of Mlle. Zhao, who slits her wrist under the wedding canopy during the ceremony, and dies in Changsha Hospital on 14 November 1919. This event takes place during a wave of suicides in China, and is recognized as symptomatic of a general state of mind. Among those to be swept away by this wave of suicides are intellectuals, for whom the attempt to create a new China, around the 4 May movement, is a call to go beyond themselves, to rise above the old personality and the old society. For the first time in the history of the country, a cry goes out for individuals and individual freedoms to transform the society. There is no tradition of individualism, no specifically Chinese vocabulary to support this liberated bourgeois revolt. In order to go full speed ahead, one needs a superego. Without it, the exacerbated tensions destroy one's equilibrium. Only those who channel

---

[1] A selection of these articles, presented and translated by Stuart Schram, appeared in French under the title *Mao Tse-tung*, texts translated and presented by Stuart Schram, Paris, A. Colin, 1963; some extracts may also be found in the article quoted above by Roxane Witke.

their newly liberated energies into the new western ideologies and attempt to adapt them to Chinese society seem capable of escaping such a predicament: these are the future Communists around Mao: Cai Chang, Zhou Enlai and his wife Deng Yingchao, etc. Women make up the second ranks of the suicides: to the traditional reasons for suicide — traditionally accepted because, as we have said, the martyr is a heroine — is added a new kind of confusion: liberalism and the feminist movement are beginning to draw converts among the great mass of women, but the social structure is not prepared. The young rebels, then, having committed themselves to far-reaching ideals of emancipation with no concrete means of realizing them, find themselves subject to the violent disapproval of those around them, and desperately seek an end to their problems by putting an end to their lives. It is impossible for me to go any further in such a psychological hypothesis without projecting onto it the western vision which I mentioned earlier.

The suicide of Mlle. Zhao came very shortly after another, that of Mlle. Zhao Ying, which Mao seems to have followed quite closely. Zhao Ying throws herself from the roof of her home in Shanghai to protest the marriage arranged by her parents, who oppose her decision to live independently and have a modern education. The posthumous publication of her letters shows, in addition, that she has been deeply influenced by Buddhist doctrine. The combination in her case of Buddhism, family pressures, and a commitment to emancipation ending in suicide, was no doubt responsible for Mao's interest in her. Mao's mother was a Buddhist; he himself, we remember, had threatened suicide when his conflict with his father was most severe; and the literature of 4 May was filled with hundreds of cases of suicide among young revolutionaries.

In all his articles inspired by the wave of suicides, Mao asserts that the pressures of family and society, the old Confucian morality, and various anachronistic social customs are diametrically opposed to individual freedom and the right of women to decide their own fate. Western commentators are surprised at the lack of psychological analysis: wouldn't personal psychological motivations and obsessions come into the picture? Some go as far as suggesting the probability of

109

'mental illness' in the case of Mlle. Zhao. Mao doesn't take this into consideration. In his revolt, he attributes all ills to society, and does not suspect that the individual in a given society internalizes much of its ethic within himself, and then falls subject to a severe inner conflict. Chinese anarchism — and such seems to be Mao's position during this period and in these nine articles on suicide in particular — struggles against an old society and believes in a better one: there is no sadistic orgy and no Nietzschean rage which would dissolve, in the individual, the very roots of a 'just society'. Such an attitude with regard to the suicide of women strikes us as rigid; but could it be a conscious effort to call a halt to despair, and provoke revolutionary action in its place? Or does it go hand-in-hand with a social and symbolic structure that has no conception of 'Christian sin' and in which the individual is not only neither 'guilty' nor 'innocent', neither 'good' nor 'evil', but simply *does not exist*, or exists only as a point of intersection of social, natural, and symbolic forces? One can't help but wonder, when faced with articles such as 'Critique of the suicide of Mlle. Zhao', 'Social Ills and Mlle. Zhao', 'Advice to Girls and Boys on the Subject of Marriage', 'The Problem of Superstition and Marriage', (against the idea of 'predestined marriages'; marriages 'made in heaven', etc.), 'Against Suicide', etc.

'He who commits suicide is not motivated by a desire for death. He does not want simply to die. Suicide, on the contrary, is the most emphatic demonstration of the will to live. The reason why people commit suicide in a society is that the society has seized their hopes and brutally crushed them. . . .'

'My position on suicide is that I reject it. . . . The goal of struggle is not to be killed by others, but rather to move toward the realization of one's true potential. If, despite all efforts, you fail to achieve this; if you sacrifice yourself to the cause and fight to the death, then you will be the most courageous person on earth, and this tragedy will make a great impression on the minds of men.'

In any case, this position is still anarchist, and strives to avoid the emergence of a metaphysical sense of individuality (Buddhist or Christian) prone to guilt and suicide, at a moment in Chinese society when feudal morality is crumbling, and the only replacement in sight is Indo-European idealism. The voluntarism of Mao's position will later be reinforced by the whole Marxist system (where 'true individualism' is replaced by the Party) and by the fight Mao himself wages against the Confucian ethic from the very earliest days of the Chinese Communist Party. This avoidance of individualism — 'wretched consciousness' — may be, as the Western observer might well deem it, a voluntarist, if not dogmatic, position. Or does it derive rather from Chinese socio-symbolic structure where precocious socialization, particularities or communication (written, spoken, gestural) and an intimate connection between relationships of production and those of reproduction may permit a considerable number of people to go beyond humanism, beyond individualism, beyond idealism? No one, in good conscience, can answer this question, which sums up the problem of China as a whole and underlines the difficulty in dealing with the problem of Chinese women in particular.

IV

Women and the Party

In 1922, about a year after its foundation, the Chinese Communist Party, on the instructions of the Third International in Moscow, creates a ministry of women, and decides to address some of its publications to the women's issue. Xiang Jingyu is the first and most eminent leader of this women's bureau of the CCP.

From the first, the women communists dissociate themselves from the women's rights movement in which most of them have participated, to defer the feminist cause to the revolutionary cause, and await the resolution of women's problems as an automatic result of the social-political transformation envisaged by the Party. This conception is the faithful reflection of Lenin's ideas and of Bolshevik Party policy on the women's movement. It provokes, in China, an interesting contradiction, due to the particular qualities of Chinse society: a contradiction that the CCP has not resolved with the same Marxist firmness, for example, that characterized its treatment of the peasant problem. The contradiction is this:

The masses of women who were first to espouse an ideological line and a political organization came from the working class. Young women concentrated in urban centres, relatively free of the control of their families (fathers and husbands: in 1940 the authorities in Guangzhou found themselves obliged to take measures against the sexual freedom of working girls and of women workers living away from their husbands), were easily won over by economic demands and a universalist policy where all exploited people, regardless of sex, could find the just solution to their misery. On the contrary, the vast majority of women — the peasants — and the most aware among the class of élite women intellectuals — the students — were sensitive mainly to family conflicts, sexual problems, and to the ideological changes that the discussion of such issues might bring about. These women, thus, were supporters of pre-Communist forms of feminism; and even when students or peasant women joined the ranks of the Party, they insisted on bringing up issues of women's rights in family and politics, since they inevitably found themselves screaming to the deaf ears of fathers and husbands — even Communist fathers and husbands.[1]

The alternatives for the Chinese Communist Party were thus clear: find a base of support either among working women, with the advantage of having a homogeneous policy (for both men and women) to build a unified movement as fast as possible; or pay attention to the feminist demands of students and peasants and find a base there — thus exposing the Party to the risk of division (men's policy/women's policy) and the inevitability of a more radical cultural revolution that would affect sexual and familial customs. Like all Communist parties of the period, the CCP chose the first line, despite the fact that the Chinese Communists were more responsible than anyone else for the establishment of a new family policy, as we shall see later on. The paradox, then, does not lie there: it lies, rather, in the fact that the CCP never bothered to make a radical change in the general conception of forces behind the revolution, even though the workers remained the 'leading force' and the intellectuals continued to furnish the vast majority of leaders.

As the article 'Critique of Confucius and the line between the two lines' in the theoretical review of the CCP, 'The Red Flag', points out: from the very foundation of the CCP, Mao's struggle against the various factions more or less affiliated with the Third International, and especially his struggle against the

---

[1]Cf. Suzette Leith, 'Chinese Women in the Early Communist Movement', in *Women in China*, op. cit. 1973.

'leftist' opportunism of Wang Ming, was principally a fight against Confucianism, and recalled, in this regard, the ideas of the 4th of May movement. The 'Report on the Investigation into the Peasant Movement at Hunan' (1927), where Mao condemns the 'three rules of conduct' (the lord guides his minister, the father guides his son, the husband guides his wife), the 'five virtues' (kindness, justice, intelligence, loyalty, adherence to ritual), and the 'four powers' (political, clan, religious, and marital) — all proposed by Mencius and Confucius — is interpreted by this magazine as an early example of Mao's struggle aaginst Confucianism. But, in fact, it is not until 1935, when the Third International relaxes its hold on the national parties, that Mao, escaping its authority, definitively asserts his conception of a peasant-led social revolution. In the 1930's as well, closer attention is paid to the problems of women and the family, as proved by the laws passed at Jiangxi. But for all that, 'the work with women' continues to be essentially regarded as subordinate to the orthodox objectives of propaganda, economic reform, and military victory over the nationalists or the Japanese. It does not give way to a new conception of the goals and methods of socialist revolution, whereas the discovery of the importance of the peasantry has created a radical change in Marxist-Leninist theory when applied to conditions in China. The theoretical and economic problems raised by the awakening of women in the first half of our century (which country and which ideology, which group, even, apart from a few limited élite circles, were and still are capable of responding?), complicated by Chinese tradition and by the internal and external threats and schisms of the nationalist, socialist, and communist movements in China, certainly are sufficient to explain the impasse of the feminist cause during that period. This situation was serious not because, as S. Leith (*op. cit*) writes, it deprived women of a 'real base of power'. It was indeed true that the only place where a Communist woman could be a leader was in 'women's issues'; in any position that did not concern feminism and was involved in politics of class rather than sex, she was subordinated to the authority of men. But this is only an incidental matter. The real question is 'what do women have to do with power?'

Power cares nothing for sexual differences: women as well as men can lend their bodies to its masque, as long as their love for the father so authorizes them. 'The other sex' is something other than power; and certainly it is not the slave who aspires to power. Knowing the condition of the other sex has nothing to do with rejoicing in a promotion to power that the master confers on you, to rule in his name. Let others have rulership; there's nothing a woman can do with it. Her role is to say to power, 'that's not it', 'that isn't enough'. An element of negation, of change, of movement. And if it's necessary to seize power for a moment to speed this movement on its course, she must never forget that this moment is unimportant, that it is an instance in the process, to be surpassed.

Therefore the failure to integrate this feminist movement with the workers' movement, in China and elsewhere, is not at all a matter of 'whether the Party will be ruled by men or women'. It is much more fundamentally a failure of the ideological struggle waged by the Communist parties themselves; perhaps the first ideological failure of the age to go unrecognized, and to open the way for those that follow. (Among them: how to get beyond bourgeois privilege without using it oneself; youth, madness; modern art, etc.)

The four women Communists who became members of the Central Committee were all sympathizers (if not militants) with the Women's Rights Movement. Xiang Jingyu, considered to be the most eminent revolutionary of her time, was graduated from the most progressive girls' school in Changsha (Hunan Province). She later founded a school where experimental methods of teaching were developed; the teacher/student hierarchy was abolished and a principle of reciprocal education and sexual equality established. Cai Chang, the sister of Mao's friend Cai Hesheng, participated in the activities of the socialist and feminist students, and, after the creation of the Communist Party, helped form study groups for women in Changsha, before leaving for France with the Study Programme led by Xiang Jingyu, who by then had become her sister-in-law. The period between 1919-1921 that this group spent in France seems to have played an important role in the formation of future women leaders: they supported the worker's movement in France, studying the theory and practice of anarchism and socialism as well as that of Marxism. Deng Yingchao was also an active student feminist: she later married Zhou Enlai, and became a member of the CCP and one of the leaders of the women's movement in the People's Republic of China. In 1922, Xiang Jingyu was named head of the women's bureau of the Central Committee. She criticized feminist groups and ideologies as individualistic when they aspired to the western bourgeois family, romantic when they called for free love, and co-opted by the bourgeois political system when, as suffragettes, they demanded political recognition. Only businesswomen escaped Xiang's censure, because they abandoned the family structure altogether; and only working women earned her praise and her political support, because of their widespread strikes. Xiang discovered that three thousand women workers from sixty textile factories, mostly in Shanghai, had gone out on strike in 1922; she decided, then, to dedicate her energies to the political education of working women. In 1923 and 1924, International Women's Day (8 March) was the occasion for a great rallying of women around the cause of labour.

At the same time, the Guomindang was involved in a rush of feminist activity, centred more on the creation of women's rights groups that supported the nationalist party than on the work with the masses envisioned by the Communists. It was the celebrated woman nationalist He Xiangning who led this campaign in Canton; during 1924-25, when Communists and Nationalists had formed a common front, Cai Chang and Deng Yingchao worked under her direction.

The call of the Party to the masses of women workers, peasants, and students, came up against traditional resistance among the general population, but also among its own male members. This is evident in the text of a resolution passed by the central committee 'On the Women's Movement' in 1926. This resolution lamented the small number of women Party members, and emphasized the importance of work with the masses without class distinction, involving all women from all ranks of society. It insisted on the role of women workers and peasants and on the necessity for publications dedicated to women. Nationalist propaganda about women also came up against resistance, largely from people in small towns and villages; thus, the School for the Education of Women, founded in Hankou by Song Qingling (the wife of Sun Yatsen, and currently the honorary head of the People's Republic of China), and extremely enthusiastic in its propaganda, created a scandal in the village when student propagandists showed up accompanied by men, or got carried away by their zeal and attempted to bob the hair of peasant women.

The failure of such feminist activism no doubt confirmed Xiang Jingyu in her tendency to abandon feminist themes in favour of the political struggles of working men and women. After spending two years in Moscow in the Communist Party schools (during which time the women's contingent of the Party was directed by Cai Chang), she became Chief of Propaganda at Hankou, where she organized the industrial proletariat of both sexes. After the break between Communists and Nationalists in 1927, Xiang continued to work underground. Arrested by the Nationalists, she defended herself during the trial by proclaiming the ideals of the French Revolution: liberty, equality, fraternity. In 1928, she was executed.

At this time, more than one and half million women from ten provinces where He Xiangning worked belonged to feminist groups, whereas, 300,000 women were members of the Communist Party.[1]

Many women were later to join the Communist Movement, during the Long March, the war against Japan, and the effort to build a socialist China after the war. But the great names of women leaders date from this period before the war. From Jiang's execution until 1949, the Central Committee of the Chinese Communist Party included only one woman: Cai Chang. By 1956, two more women had been appointed: Deng Yingchao, the wife of Zhou Enlai, and Chen Shaoming, an active militant in the anti-Japanese resistance. Mao's third wife, Jiang Qing (Chiang Ching), who arrived in Yenan as a young actress sympathizing with the Communists, did not become a member of the Central Committee until the Cultural Revolution was already on the way. The two famous Song

---

[1]S. Leith, *op. cit.*

sisters of Guomindang both made their political debuts during that period: one married Sun Yatsen, and then became honorary Chairman of China beside Mao; the other married Jiang Jieshi (Chiang Kai-shek). The biographies of the 'great women' of modern China in Helen Foster Snow's book (Mouton 1967) read almost like romantic fiction. Marked by the bourgeois liberation, by the ideas of 4th May, by the Chinese 'suffragette' movement, by the West whose languages they frequently spoke (whether or not they were daughters of the upper classes), they wanted to rise above their condition as women by means of a proletarian universalism, in which the cause of women was but one among many; and they continued to pursue that cause carefully, modestly, and as much or as little as circumstance and the urgent task of liberating, feeding, and educating this immense nation would permit.

At first a suffragette feminism, then an objective of communism, the Chinese women's liberation movement becomes the 'spirit of the laws' from the 1930's onwards. The *Civil Code* of Guomindang includes a *Family Law* (books four and five) of 5 May 1931, which insures, among other things the equality of the sexes and the conclusion of marriage and divorce by mutual consent. The patriarchal family is abolished, and the bourgeoisie replaces it, as is evident from the provision on private property: both parties retain ownership of their goods, but the husband manages them. In the Communist legislation of the Jiangxi Soviet in 1930, however, the abolition of the ancient feudal family is not only more radically formulated, but infinitely more effective: whereas the Guomindang law remains on paper, the Jiangxi law is immediately enforced on the millions of men and women in the region.

A report by Mao on 10 June 1922 on the 'current situation' already defines the image that Chinese communism has of society, an image we have heard repeated many times in China, even this year: having lived for thousands of years under feudalism, China-between-the-two-wars is a 'semi-feudal, semi-bourgeois' or a 'semi-feudal, semi-colonial' country. The proletarian liberation will consequently have to be a liberation from patriarchal structures as well; therefore, a liberation from paternal power. As a Japanese Marxist has said, in a country where the immense majority of the proletariat is in the country-side, the liberation of the rural proletariat is equivalent to a liberation from the authority of the father.[1]

This would tend to explain Mao's position in his 'Report on an Investigation into The Peasant Movement at Hunan' (made in 1927, published in his *Selected Works*, Peking 1966, and in an original version by Stuart Schram, A. Colin, 1963).

On the one hand, Mao asserts the necessity for three kinds of struggle: against political power, against clan power, and against theocratic power. For women, a fourth area of struggle must be added: against the power of their husbands. But a passage which was deleted from the final report shows that Mao had also recognized this:

> . . . In sexual matters, the poor peasant women have a good deal of freedom. In the villages, triangular and multilateral relationships are practically universal among the poor peasantry.

Mao warns the peasants against being overly hasty in abolishing the old morality: the requirement for chastity in a woman is so fundamentally engrained in the peasant mentality that to attack it (as part of the attack on Confucianism) might result in the very destruction of peasant relationships.

> It must be the peasants themselves who remove the idols, who break the ancestral tablets, and who destroy the temples of women who did not wish to survive their husbands, and the shrines built to honour chaste wives and faithful widows.

This prudence does not keep Mao, the Chairman of the Jiangxi Soviet, from promoting a *Marriage Decree* (1930) which continues to astonish specialists in its uniqueness among the annals of world jurisprudence.

The text of the *Decree* says overtly that:

> men without wives may take the liberty of finding a

---

[1]Cf. Nobory Niida, *Law of Slave and Self, Research in the History of Chinese Law*, v. 3, Tokyo 1962.

wife as quickly as possible, and women without husbands may take the liberty of finding a husband as quickly as possible.

The term 'take the liberty' is an ungrammatical usage, verbal rather than nominative, 'zi you', 'Liberty'. One could translate it more faithfully by:

> men without wives should 'pick up' a woman as soon as possible.[1]

It goes without saying that this Decree had instant results. As Hu Chi-hsi notes, the Jiangxi Soviet thus became the testing ground for a new morality, and not only a new mode of production (collectivization, creation of co-operatives, etc.). What the CCP does not dare promote on an ideological basis during the 'twenties and 'thirties begins to take effect once the party comes to power, even if in only a single region of China. The Chinese Communist Revolution from that time on shows a face that is unknown among communists in power in the West, a face that war against Japan, the Civil War, and, afterward, the fallout from western history (fascism, Stalinism, American imperialism) will veil once more.

Other legislative provisions made at Jiangxi confirm and amplify this Decree. The *Plenum* of the Central Committee of the Chinese Communist Party of 3 March 1931 draws up a *Plan of Action on the Women's Issue*, where Maoist hostility to working-class sectarianism during the early days of the CCP is obvious. The *Plan* asserts that

> soviet political principles must be applied to women in order to destroy the legal norms of the old society, to oppose the exploitative relationships of the feudal family, etc. . . . , to guarantee women's equality with men and permit them to acquire civil rights.

Not wishing to isolate the women's movement from the main-

---

[1]Cf. Hu Chi-hsi, 'Mao, la revolution, et la question sexuelle', in *Revue Française de Sciences politiques*, February 1973, *Tel Quel*, n. 59, 1974.

stream of the revolutionary movement, the *Plan* declares itself against 'absolute freedom of marriage' but for 'freedom', which means: there will be no forced feudal or bourgeois marriage, but the institution of marriage itself will not be abolished.

The *Constitution* of November, 1931, goes one step further, suggesting the possibility of a *society without the family*:

> Freedom of marriage is recognized and measures for the protection of women will assure them the necessary material means *to dissolve the family bond* stage by stage, and fully participate in cultural, political, and economic life. (Italics mine.)

In this particular stage, a *Marriage Resolution* follows the *Constitution* and assures an unprecedented freedom to women. They are given advantages which surpass those accorded to men. The way is thus opened to eliminate — if not the family — at least the patriarchal clan. Among the provisions of this *Marriage Regulation* of 1931, which was extremely attractive to feminine psychology in the Chinese Soviet, there was one authorizing free choice of spouse and prohibiting marriage between relatives through the fifth generation, as well as between so-called 'piao' cousins (i.e. 'relatives of the same generation other than those to whom one is connected exclusively by males' — cousins, then, in the maternal lineage. This is an allusion to marriage with the maternal cousin, daughter of the mother's brother, of which we have spoken above, and which was a survival of the maternal right in the patrilinear family. That such a custom should be mentioned in the law means that it must still have been practised to a considerable degree). This provision strikes a blow at the system of clan isolation by arranged marriage between relatives: no more blood unity, no more economic and political unity tending to keep the clan from participating in inter-familial social relationships. The provision concerning divorce is extremely important: completely 'free', divorce assures the economic security of the woman alone (the husband is responsible for the children, he must pay alimony to the wife, etc.). In the perhaps over-zealous desire to pay reparation for millenia of injustice, divorce is made highly unattractive to men and extremely appealing to women. One final blow to the family: the *Regulation* abolishes the distinction between legitimate and illegitimate children. Let us remember that it was not until very recently that French law so delicately did the same.

A final Jiangxi document, the *Marriage Law* of April 1934, follows the general direction of the *Regulation*, with certain additions. Boys of twenty and girls of eighteen have the right to marry. Their choice is free and sovereign. Divorce is also free, but both marriage and divorce must be declared before the authorities. This is the famous 'registration', on which Mao personally insists, and which is proposed as a means of protecting women against the abuses of patriarchal mores, and at the same time avoiding anarchy and assuring the right of the State to intervene in relationships of reproduction. Thus, to warn against secrecy and to congratulate himself on the 'registration' Mao writes in 1934:

> In the course of the four and a half years of Communist rule, one woman out of one hundred (in the canton of Changgang, Xingguo district) was married three times. Before the arrival of the communists, on the other hand fifty per cent of the women in the canton were carrying on secret love affairs. Following the establishment of soviet power, this figure has fallen by ten per cent. . . . The reasons for this are: first, the land reform movement; second, freedom of marriage and divorce; third, the importance of time dedicated to revolutionary activity.[1]

The 1934 law adds the following refinements to the Regulation of 1931: polyandry, as well as polygamy, is prohibited; marriage between relatives is forbidden through the third generation; *de facto* marriages — that is, where the couples have not registered with the authorities, are recognized. An end is put to the parasitism of divorced women, who were able to take advantage of the earlier Regulation: children are henceforth in the custody of the mother, though the father must contribute to their support; the divorced husband does not support

---

[1]Quoted by Hu Chi-hsi, *op. cit.*

his wife unless she is judged incapable of working; a soldier's wife cannot obtain a divorce without the consent of her husband, and only after four years of marriage or a certain period of 'trial reconciliation'. Such restrictions, however, do not contradict the 'spirit of the law', which aims at the ultimate dissolution of the family.

Traditional Chinese law had never been concerned with 'individual freedom'. At the very most, it recognized the freedom of a group; but that group was most often the nation itself. The new legislative provisions of the Chinese Communist Party seems to act in a different spirit, which may be traced to Sun Yatsen in its recognition of free personal choice and in the worth it accords to the 'other half of the sky' — women. (It is also true that the 1926 Matrimonial Code of the USSR is faithful to this libertarian tendency, before the restrictions of 1937, 1939, and 1944, which end up imposing the Cult of the Family). In comparison to western legislation, the Chinese code is extremely concise: there are only twenty-three articles in the *Regulation* of 1931. In addition, the methods of registering marriage and divorce are not specified. As M. J. Meijer says in *Marriage Law and Policy in the People's Republic of China*,[1] the goal of Communist legislation has never been to cover all the problems of marriage and the family, but only to establish general guidelines for freedom and for the protection of the most disadvantaged (women and children), and to provide punitive measures not so much against those who prevent the emergence of a new conception of the family as against those who impede the broad social transformation that such a conception would be largely responsible for. In other words, the family matters very little in these legislative provisions, which, in any case, are not called 'family laws', but rather 'marriage laws'. They do not deal with family relationships. It is as if this 'microcosm of society' were simply not the concern of the Jiangxi lawmaker; he does not care to lay down the rules for its functioning, nor does it seem to interest him in the least. What interests him are the individuals to whom freedom of economic and political action must be given:

---

[1]Hong Kong University Press, 1971, p. 43.

123

thus, *marriage* — and not the family — is an intermediary measure which should permit the individual to break off his indenture to the patriarchal feudal family, in order to become part of something far superior to the family: communist society and its sub-divisions, the fundamental politico-economic units.

Finally, we must emphasize that the war against Japan and the civil war itself, which scattered families throughout the country and destroyed their economic base, played a major role in the dissolution of old family customs, and thus helped accomplish the goal of the decrees and the propaganda of the political and ideological revolution.

It is nonetheless true that the matrimonial law does not entirely achieve its goals during this period, not only because of certain abuses in local enforcement of the Jiangxi legislation (wives are forced to 'be free', widows to remarry within five days, etc.); but especially because of the lack of real political and economic independence for women. Mao calls attention to this in a report given before the National Congress of Soviets in March, 1934, where he says that the new system of marriage 'is one of the greatest victories in the history of mankind', but adds that freedom of marriage will be guaranteed only when the man and the woman have both political and economic freedom (with political freedom being the first priority).

However, as is often the case in Chinese history and in the history of the CCP in particular, after a 'yin victory' comes a 'yang victory'. The period that follows, that of the Long March from the south to the northwestern corner of China, is a period of tremendous human effort: stoicism and superego replace the experimentation of a new society in which sexual revolution, along with economic reform, was to have been a motivating force. The condtions of war are not alone in dictating this change in policy: the more stringent, puritanical, Confucian 'mores' of northwest China play an equally important role. After an initial attempt in 1936 to enforce the Jiangxi *Marriage Law* in the northwest, the CCP changes its line and makes some concessions. For the first time, the preservation of the family is assured, and concern is shown for the relationship between the married couple. A strict morality is demanded of wives, rules are made regarding the possession of private property by husband or wife, and 'grounds' are introduced for divorce, which thus ceases to be 'free'.

Women participate considerably in the event at Yenan. Many women are in the army, and receive military training. Others undertake industrial or agricultural work. Still others are involved in the ideological sector: they spread propaganda among the soldiers and the civilian population. For the female population of the northwest, the Party proposes communist youth leagues, anti-Japanese brigades.[1] To mobilize all the available female forces, while taking their particular abilities into account, it draws up an order in January 1936:

> To mobilize women, boys, and old men to participate in spring planting and cultivation, each according to his ability to carry on either a principal or an auxiliary task in the labour process of production. For example, 'large feet,' [natural feet] and young women should be mobilized to organize production-teaching corps, with tasks varying from land clearance up to the main tasks of agricultural production itself. 'Small feet' [bound feet], young boys, and old men must be mobilized to help in weed-pulling, collecting dung, and for other auxiliary tasks.[2]

This period of effort and austerity does not seem propitious for the considerations of women's rights or free love, and the speech Mao makes at Yenan on art and literature bears this out. He criticizes his comrades 'who are seeking an abstract love, beyond class distinctions'. Nonetheless, even in this period, the grottos of Yenan ring with the theme of women and love, as the American journalist Agnes Smedley has remarked in her admirable study, *The Battle Hymn of China*.[3] The people poke gentle fun at an austere ascetic leader, who 'is married only to the Revolution' — which gives him an ulcer. They joke while listening to a nationalist radio broadcast that accuses the Communists of raping the women and girls

---

[1] Cf. Edgar Snow, *Red Star over China*, 1965.
[2] Snow, *Red Star over China*, p. 222.
[3] London, Victor Gollancz, Ltd., 1944.

of the regions they conquer: we must remember, that to destroy the Jiangxi Soviet, Chiang Kai-shek launched not only a military offensive, but the 'New Life Movement' (1943), which flattered the rural conservativism, exalted Confucian virtue, and accused the communists of wanting to 'collectivize' women. Whereas Mao, just separated from his second wife He Zezhen, who has gone off to Moscow, asks Smedley if she has ever loved a man, and why; and wants her to tell him what love means to her.

The puritanism of Yenan did have its limits, however, at least at first. Smedley organized dancing lessons in which Zhou Enlai and Zhu De, among others, participated. Zhu, in the face of an extremely negative reaction among certain Chinese women who felt that the 'foreigner was corrupting the army', proclaimed, 'All my life I have fought against feudalism; I'm not going to stop now!'

Some women from this northwestern region, through local women's associations, actively helped the Communists, and were among the most outspoken in exposing the abuses of power on the part of those who would later be called 'the rotten eggs'. An old peasant woman of 68, Mother Cai, begged Smedley to tell western women how women in China were fighting for their emancipation, adding: 'You express the high spirit of womanhood in your willingness to eat bitterness with us.'[1]

In many subsequent documents concerning the policy of working on women's issues in anti-Japanese bases and, later, in the liberated zones, we find that the CCP is concerned about adapting its propaganda to the particularities of feminine psychology. These documents, drawn up, no doubt, with the active participation of Cai Chang and Deng Yingchao, are largely self-critiques. The propaganda of the Chinese Communist Party, they say, in its essentially economic and class-oriented or directly political thrust,

> has not taken into account the family responsibilities of women, their physiological limitations, and their difficult lives.

---

[1]Smedley, *The Battle Hymn of China*, p. 192.

The organizations of the party function for their own benefit, and not for women: too many meetings, too many unnecessary mobilization campaigns. An effort must be made, the women say, to

> encourage women to change the old customs like foot-binding and neglect of personal hygiene, which injuire their health and affect their work.[1]

A testament to the reticence of women before the abrupt style of communist propaganda? A harking back to the feminist principles of 4 May and the Jiangxi Soviet? Both, doubtless; but it is significant that it is after a confrontation with the feminine masses that some doubt arises as to the effectiveness of an ideology centered wholly on economics, and under-estimating the needs and desires of 'the people'. Additional declarations, like that on the 'work with women' in the rural regions of the liberated zones (December 1948) take up the same theme: the women are not participating enough, the propaganda is too voluntarist.

One year later, Deng Yingchao writes a report on the tasks of the women's movement, in which she sees an important ally for the construction of the new China and in the fight against feudal ideology. She does not neglect the specifically feminine issues of children, hygiene, body care. These principles are taken up by the First Congress of Chinese Women, on 1 April, 1949, and in its *Resolution on Present Objectives of the Women's Movement in China*. Here, too, there is little concern for the family; but that is the only echo of the legislation of Jiangxi. The document ranges from discussions of women and their right to freedom and equality, to the necessity for con-structing a socialist state. Already the accent has changed from 'freedom of marriage' to the *effort* that will be demanded of 'the other half of the sky' to lay the foundation for a new mode of production.

---

[1]Cf. *Decision of the Central Committee of the Chinese Communist Party on the present policy on women in anti-Japanese bases*, 26 February 1943, in *Documents of the Women's Movement in China*, Peking, 1950.

The Marriage Law (1905). Love and Demography. Women in Command.

The Chinese feudal family was, as we have seen, a kinship unit built around the dominant symbolic function of the father; it was an economic unit as well. Thus, it is understandable that a single blow, *The Marriage Law*, would suffice to get rid of both the old economy and the old ideology. In Russia, the Leninist decree on land left the ideological problem open: ecclesiastical authority surpassed even that of the 'zadruga', and an atheistic, anti-church campaign was called for. As M. J. Meijer quite aptly remarks, in China the church was the family. To attack the patriarchal family, then, was to attack the foundation of the economy *and* of the ideology — their point of intersection, their support. The policy of agrarian reform turned the Chinese socialist revolution — which had begun with purely economic goals in mind — into an anti-patriarchal revolt. And a revolution against the father meant a women's revolution. The problem was, how far would it be carried? At Jiangxi, when the necessity was to *destroy* the old rather than to *construct* the new, it was possible to question authority and to prophesy the disappearance of the family. After the Long March, after the war, during the Cold War, when the first priority was to build a new regime, the maintenance of some inviolable authority seemed to be necessary: women and the family could only aspire to wield it equally with men. Hence, the two objectives of the *Marriage Law*:

down with the old feudal family, up with responsibility for women. A new enemy is added to the list: 'bourgeois morality', a catch-all term for all things other than patriarchal puritanism which would oppose family stability and the potential for women to fulfill their responsibilities as mothers and citizens (hence: adultery, various forms of deception with money and power, prostitution, etc.).

The *Marriage Law* is thus preceded by the Legal Provisions for Agrarian Reform (1947). Following Marxist theory, the construction of the new country had to begin at the bottom. But from the first attempts to enforce the *Provisions* it becomes clear that land reform is family reform, and pits itself against all the old economic and ideological structures. Numerous voices, especially in the Women's Associations, cry out to demand that women's issues and the fight against the *jia* be made a priority. The Chinese Communist Party hears them, and listens 'so as not to cut itself off from the masses'; but once more it subordinates them to an economic issue — land reform, which seems more urgent and, in any case, is one of the chief demands of the feminists. The result is that the grievances of women against the family become a motivating force behind the new economic structures, and, in some places, even the principal force in agrarian reform. Xiu Guang, the deputy chairwoman of the Revolutionary Committee west of Peking sums up this period in the following way:

'At that time, marriage, medical care for women and children, and other things were among the urgent problems in Zhaojiazhuang (the region where Xiu Guang worked in 1947). Many peasant women, therefore, proposed that our association 'be exclusively concerned with the well-being of women', and said, 'let the peasant's union take care of land reform'. At the close of a discussion among the members of the Women's Association, it was unanimously agreed that the association should look out for the immediate interests of women, even at the risk of 'cutting itself off from the masses', since the accomplishment of the central task of the revolution, i.e. agrarian reform, was still more important. . . . Women were very active in the land reform movement. . . . In the reform, each poor peasant received a piece of land. To emphasize the equality of men and women, women peasants received their own deeds, or had their names inscribed on the family deeds. Many of these women had previously been known merely as 'Housewife of the such-and-such house', or 'Mother of So-and-So'. Now for the first time they were called by their own names.[1]

After a year and five months of preparation, through discussions among the people and in the legislative bodies and the women's organizations, the *Marriage Law* was announced by Mao on 1 May 1950, and adopted by the government and the Political Consultation Congress of the Chinese People on 1 December 1951. The first article sets forth its general principle:

> The arbitrary and compulsory feudal marriage system, which is based on the superiority of men over women, and which ignores the interests of children, is abolished. The 'New Democratic Marriage System', based on free choice of partners, on monogamy, on equal rights for both sexes and on protection of the lawful interests of women and children, shall be put into effect.

Once more, compared to bourgeois legislation, the *Marriage Law* is rather a moral code than a law. It lacks a *text*: differentiations, specifications, guidelines for the consideration of various cases and situations. This lack leaves the door open for interpretation, and, thus, for an uncontrollable bureaucracy. (Bourgeois bureaucracy, on the other hand, is subject to an intricately detailed law. The simple result is that, if socialist law is more egalitarian, bourgeois law does a better job of guaranteeing rights.) Conversely, if a more or less free interpretation is opened to the masses, law and jurisdiction cease to exist and yield to a sort of popular morality where whoever has the upper hand will win. The choice here necessarily falls somewhere between bureaucracy and mob rule. The fate of democracy, thus, depends on the possibility of the masses to go

---

[1] *La Chine en construction*, March 1973.

against the tide — with all the arbitrary risks that that implies.

With these limitations, which are the limitations of socialist legislation, *the Marriage Law accords more rights to women than bourgeois law could do.*

First, husband and wife have equal status in the family. Chinese law does not recognize a 'head of household'. Article VII says:

> Husband and wife are companions living together, and shall enjoy equal status in the home.

Next this *Law* gives more advantages to women than western legislation does. Thus, not only may a woman retain her maiden name (article XI) after marriage, but her children have the right to take her name rather than her husband's. (This last provision, formulated not by the *Law*, but by subsequent decisions, is currently considered to be part of the *Marriage Law*). One's own name, as we have said, is the symbolic equivalent of unity and power in a society: from whence its imagined 'virile' and 'phallic' value. Thus, to authorize women to keep their own names not only strikes a blow at patrilinear descent (as Xiu Guang noted above); it elevates women at the same time to symbolic power. This 'virilization', this 'phallicization' of women, can help them to leave the household, the bedchamber, and the more or less psychotic sexuality where they traditionally take refuge with more or less pleasure and profit: a tonic against psychosis and at the same time against the cultural, political, and economic backwardness of the female population. But, in fact, to acknowledge a woman's real name (i.e. her father's name) is only the first step, and it will have no impact on patriarchal society unless it is followed by another: the possibility for the woman to give herself a 'symbolic name', i.e. a 'personality' of her own, an autonomous voice, a specific social function. In China, the question has only been asked. But it has been asked with perhaps more clarity than in the West, because Confucian patriarchy, more than monotheistic patriarchy, has been haunted by the mother, by her sexuality, and by her function as the inversion of power. It is possible, consequently, that the effects of this 'right to use her (father's) name' are not the same for a western woman

131

and for a Chinese. A western woman with her own (father's) name — when this name is recognized as belonging to her, as being the mark of her own symbolic worth — finds herself unmistakably virilized by it, and thus achieves the status of 'free autonomous sexless individual', if not the equivalent of power and dominance, the phallus itself. By identification and projection, perhaps, we fear the same effect on Chinese women. I remember my own distrust — and even more so that of the men in our group — before Chinese women, headmistresses of schools or factory managers, women with names and power. But if the symbolic and libidinous organization of the Chinese society is one where the cleavage (private erotic universe/ communal universe of power) is more radical than in our own, it is also an organization in which 'the erotic' is less repressed (cf. the survival of the matriarchy until Confucian times) and — above all — socialized. Granted, such socialization is secret, esoteric, and 'underground', in relation to official morality; but it is no less universal, no less widespread through the culture (cf. Taoism or Chinese Buddhism). It is possible that, in such a society, the fact that you use your own name does not necessarily make you an 'asexual metaphysical individual entity'. Rather, it permits you to function as an element — as a graphic mark in a network of meanings — in the realms of both impulse and law. An element constantly wooed by what, for us, is psychosis — and constantly out of its grasp.

Other advantages provided by the *Law* seem theoretically to favour a status for Chinese women in which they are not free individuals, but active elements in sexual pleasure (which they have always been), and in production (which they are beginning to be). Thus, a man does not have the right to apply for divorce during his wife's pregnancy and until a year after the child has been born; but the wife may (Article XVIII). After the divorce, the mother normally gets custody of a nursing child (in case the husband contests it, the decision is made 'in the interests of the child' [Article XX]).

Finally, the *Marriage Law* takes the labour of the housewife into account. Not only is housework considered socially valuable and equal to any other kind of work; not only is an effort made to lighten it (by encouraging men to participate in household chores and by creating communal dining halls and nurseries, etc.); but a form of compensation for the women's housework is provided by article X, which states that the wife's work in the home is equal to the husband's outside the home, and entitles the wife to an equal share in the possession of family property. In the absense of private property or even of the sort of 'marriage contract' that regulates family property under French law, for example, this clause is of considerable advantage to the housewife: it eliminates the difference between productive and non-productive work, gives property to one who does not produce consumer goods, and thereby provides a certain economic base for the ideological claims for freedom and autonomy of those engaged in so-called 'women's work', (cooking, cleaning, child care, etc.) and not only for those women who serve as labourers in a 'socialist economy'. Given that even in the economic systems of the most industrialized societies housework continues to absorb the energies of the overwhelming majority of women (all that mechanization does not replace domestic workers, who grow more and more scarce), the western housewife, contrary to the Chinese, remains the 'household proletariat', so long as the law (perhaps temporary and accompanied by an intense ideological campaign which, in the long run, will make such legislation unnecessary) fails to provide, in the marriage contract or elsewhere, compensation for housework.

The family in which the Chinese woman enjoys this status is a stable institution in itself, that varies in degree with the various political and economic phases of Chinese socialism. Nevertheless, the *Law*, as well as the interpretations we heard of it during our journey, gives the impression that one is dealing with a transient institution. In the *Law*, this impression is given particularly by the ease with which a divorce may be obtained: the divorce is a formal recognition of a state that already exists, and is granted immediately where both parties consent and after an attempt at reconciliation if only one party desires it. The facility of divorce has been such that the *Marriage Law* has been commonly known by the people as 'The Divorce Law'. In 1950, 186,167 divorces were registered. One year later, the figures rose sharply: 409,500. Two years later: 823,000. After 1956, the figures rose into the millions.

Currently, divorce is not nearly as easy, or as common. In a people's commune near Nanking, Tong Jin (the *Bronze Well*), which has 30,000 inhabitants, there has been only one divorce in eight years since the Cultural Revolution: because, as He Lixian, the deputy chairwoman of the administrative committee says: 'Since husband and wife choose each other freely, and have no reason to quarrel over property, there is no serious motive for divorce that can't be patched up by a discussion with their comrades.' But even if, at the moment, the family is being maintained by creating obstacles to divorce, there is nothing to indicate that the nuclear family itself is being preserved as the basic unit of the new society. Two conceptions of the family remain consistent throughout the fluctuations of successive campaigns: it is a *biological boundary* and an *educational institution*. The *Marriage Law* stipulates that:

> the blood ties between parents and children are not dissolved even after the divorce of the parents. (Article XX)

Zhao Guangwu, professor of philosophy and dean of the department of dialectical materialism at the University of Peking, told us that:

> the form of the family may change throughout history, but the family itself will never disappear because blood ties will never disappear.

Is it impossible to imagine that the species can propagate itself without the institution of the family? or is the institution of the family already considered void of political and psychological meaning, since society can assume all of its functions at some point or other, and we already understand 'family' to mean the pure and simple act of reproduction? By maintaining the family, then, does society simply give itself a means of controlling its rate of growth? A means of control called 'family' today, but something else tomorrow? Whereas the true circumstances of education, ethics, and production will have nothing to do with biological reproduction? But even if that were possible, who or what would replace this chamber of the imagination — fantasies, feelings, psychology — that is the family today, in all its modes of production and in all the various religious systems it reflects? Will this zone of fantasy simply disappear, or be reabsorbed into the society? Will its potential be immediately invested in politics, in the community — with all the passion and all the risks that that implies? In any case, we are suspicious; no one — neither here nor in China — is ready for that just yet.

In comparison with pre-Liberation legislation, the *Marriage Law* attests to a certain 'family spirit', even while vigorously defending the rights of women and going further than the Jiangxi Soviet in authorizing women to keep their own names and give them to their children. Henceforth an effort will be made to build 'a new kind of family', different from the bourgeois and feudal families. Three characteristics essential to this new family are prescribed:

(1) The foundations of this family are 'ethical', rather than economic. The Law insists on the equality of husband and wife, 'companions living together', who are duty bound to love each other, to such a point that in modern China one does not say 'husband' or 'wife', but 'my beloved' — something which brings a smile to the faces of Chinese brought up before this proclamation. This accent on the ethical bond does not, however, ignore the economic: the *Law* states that parents and children have the right to inherit each other's property;

(2) A third person comes into the man/woman relationship: the child, who has the right to care and education, and the duty to help his parents;

(3) The *Law* does not mention *de facto* marriages, but requires that all conjugal unions be registered: a symbolic protest against the old feudal marriage arranged by the parents, but also an acknowledgement of popular power, since one presents oneself as 'married' before the people. Divorce is by mutual consent, or after an attempt at reconciliation if only one of the parties desires it. It, too, must be registered with the authorities. If custody of the children is granted by the people's court to the mother, the father is responsible for all or part of the expense of

the child's care and education.

Of particular interest is Article VIII, which implies that the family is not considered simply in itself, but as an intermediate link between individuals and the policy of the socialist community. The family is a sort of school, a cell for the socialist education of the children and the propagation of the socialist ethic; but it does not exist of and for itself.

> (Article VIII): Husband and wife are in duty bound to love, respect, assist, and look after each other; to live in harmony; to engage in productive work; to care for their children; and to strive jointly for the welfare of the family and for the building of the new society.

During our journey, the teachers at the Changjianlu Secondary School in Nanking told us that three factors are responsible for the education of the children: the family, the school, and society. One can easily imagine that the most fundamental body, the family, performs the necessary educational function, so that the school, as a supplement to the family, intervenes only to complete what the family is incapable of doing because of present gaps or limitations in knowledge: to teach the child maths, for example. This educative function of the family seems to be more important than its reproductive function. For example, divorce on grounds of barrenness or physical defects in the woman is refused.[1] With the maintenance of the family, albeit for let us say 'extra-familial reasons', a strict morality comes along. The reticence of peasants and soldiers is cited to justify the policy against 'free' love and marriage; but so is the fact that such freedoms may undermine the security of women and children in a society where the patriarchal mentality co-exists with the vestiges of colonialist bourgeois morality. This strictness, though, is not carried to puritanical extremes: bigamy is punished, but adultery is not, since it is considered to result from a conflict of opinion that can be resolved by propaganda for communist morality. Evidently, in 1950 (and even afterward), the matter

---

[1]*Renmin Ribao*, 27 December 1951, quoted by Meijer, p. 109.

of 'sex education' or analysis of sexuality itself never comes up. The new society seems drunk on its new freedom of choice in sexual partner, and plunges into a wave of divorce. Women are the overwhelming majority to apply: between 1950-1952 92.4% in some regions. The coincidence of goals of the *Marriage Law* and the *Land Reform Act* seems to give impetus to this wave: the clan system is deprived of its economic base by the reform, women are given an equal share in property, and the fight against superstition undermines the patriarchy.

Now, however, as at the turn of the century during the blaze of the suffragettes, a wave of women suicides follows the wave of divorces: 70,000-80,000 women take their own lives. One of the contributing factors seems to be the opposition to divorce in certain rural areas: the divorcee is subjected to the hostility of her neighbours, and the woman seeking divorce is frequently turned down by the local cadre, who imposes arbitrary restrictions. (In other areas, though, women obtain divorces more easily than men; their motives are interpreted as anti-feudal, whereas men are suspected of acting from a 'petit bourgeois mentality'.

In any case, if these suicides indicate a crisis, it is indeed a 'crisis of transition' (too brutal?) from the feudal family to 'another' family — but not in the least a crisis of the principle of the family itself. Here we are touching on the fundamental difference between the family system and the status of women in the West, and the family system and the status of women in China. Here, divorce, contraception, and 'sexual freedom' signal the breakdown of the family: impossible as an institution, it is channeled into the game that each individual member plays in the field of power and language. In China, the family is not undergoing a crisis that will end in its disappearance in a wider symbolic and economic sphere. Our psychological 'family' has never existed in China, as we have seen; the Chinese family, rather, has always been a symbolic and economic contract. Therefore, it does not go through 'crises'; it simply draws up a new contract. A new symbolic unit of production is deemed superior to the clan, and so replaces it; and therefore the *jia* loses most of the reasons for its existence that had been furnished by Confucianism, the Chinese 'Church'.

But what about the 'other' aspect of family life, the 'art of the bedchamber', the 'sex manuals' of the Taoists we spoke of earlier? To keep them in the shadow of the new political ethic of the modern family, to refuse to deal with them — is this simply a matter of postponement, following the logic that 'you can't take care of everything at once'? Or is this cleavage (sexual life on the one hand, the political ethic on the other) a mark of civilization, a deliberate regulation of social taboo, sublimation, sexual pleasure — a regulation no worse, and perhaps more successful, than many others? Or is it a legacy from Confucianism that still endures, even if the *content* of this new morality is no longer the same? But then, if the Confucian *form* persists under this new *content*, how far can one get in the fight against Confucius? One thing is certain: the *Marriage Law* (and, as we shall see, its subsequent interpretations) does not seek to damage the *principle* of the family, but to preserve it as a nucleus of biological reproduction (reservoir of the race) and, implicitly, as a refuge for eroticism — so long as no one says so. Therefore, the family is maintained as an intermediary between the desires and the organisms of political and economic power, in which and through which the family as an instance disappears. Disappears, but not without having tapped, trained, modelled, educated all the instinctive and symbolic capacities of its members. Mistress of this education from time immemorial, the Chinese woman hereafter assumes a position of leadership in these units of economic and political power. A supremacy without historical precedent.

* * *

The problems encountered in enforcing the *Law*, coupled to the general orientation of the regime toward increasing production, may be considered responsible for a change in attitude toward the family from 1953 on. A general directive of 1 February 1953 signed by Zhou Enlai emphasizes 'conjugal happiness', and says nothing further about problems due to vestiges of feudalism. The directive is followed by a mass movement reflected in the press. Couples tell the secrets of their marital success. At the same time, feeling seems to run more against *bourgeois* morality than feudalism: the rush of divorces is considered 'bourgeois', as are the groups of little provincial middle-class couples banding together to acquire more property, the substitution of economic considerations (worthy profession, important job, etc.) for love in determining marriage partners, disrespect for parents, adultery, concubinage, etc. Reading these articles gives one the impression that the socialist ethic is in danger of being carried away by two currents: first, a hard-to-control sexuality that transgresses the law, and, second, a trend toward profiteering and the accumulation of private wealth, which takes advantage of the new provisions in which collectivization still leaves a certain margin for individual enterprise. In the face of these two dangers, the Jiangxi type of experiment with freedom is only a memory: the new reality calls for the superego rather than the libido of the revolution.

The campaign against bourgeois thought is launched again in 1956-57, in a more sophisticated way. Women are advised against coquettishness, and encouraged to develop their intellects, as if the ultimate goal were to remove them from the realm of seduction and reproduction where they were only too happy to remain, and point them in the direction of the socialist effort. Would women resist this appeal to leave the hearth and come into a social life beyond the family? In any case, the texts incite them to educate themselves intellectually and politically; but the pre-Liberation spirit that criticized an over-stereotyped propaganda, unsympathetic to the needs and desires of women, is nowhere to be found.

Polygamy, adultery, and pandering are not only clearly discouraged by communist morality — they are sharply condemned. Those who take advantage of their social and political positions to institute mores contrary to the ethic proclaimed in the Marriage Law are particularly denounced. Should we assume that some cadres took advantage of their roles to act like feudal lords, masters of land and women? A poster from 1 March 1956, photographed by some Westerners, proclaims that the people's court of Guilin, in the south, has imposed the death penalty on a teacher convicted of having raped several of his students.

•   •   •

The first censuses taken in the People's Republic of China, showing that the population (in 1958) was easily 600,000,000, had at first sparked the enthusiasm of the leaders, confident that such massive human forces would triumphantly realize the new economy and the new ideology. The problem of commanding the economic resources necessary to sustain such a population was quickly apparent: as early as 1956, a campaign was launched to limit the number of births, 'to diminish the consumption of non-productive persons during this period while we are building a socialist state'. Measures are taken to sterilize both men and women, as well as to encourage abortion (rather widely practised in the past by primitive means, along with infanticide among the poor) and contraception. This family planning was to put an end to the age where 'one saw thousands of pregnant women, and never once heard the laughter of children'. It came up against violent resistance, not only on the part of men who did not want to be sterilized, but also from many women, who still considered their principal worth to lie in their wombs, and resented any interference in their sexual affairs. The raising of the 'desirable' age for marriage (now 28 for men, 25 for women), without being made law, became an ideological demand and was generally adhered to; its purpose was also to lower the birth rate. Another aspect of the campaign was the encouragement of small families, two children being the ideal. All the officials — regardless of rank — whom we encountered even in the Chinese countryside had families of two or three children at the most. The situation is still quite different among the general rural populace, despite the indisputable success of family planning in recent years. Thus, He Lixian, vice-chair-woman of the popular commune *Bronze Well* near Nanking, admitted to us that the only serious ideological problems of the village concern the survival of superstitions that are crystallized, for her, in the desire to produce male children and in the various rituals performed to obtain them or to celebrate their arrival in the world.

Today, in fact, in all the production units of China (people's communes and factories) and in neighbourhoods as well, courses are organised to encourage family planning and to

140

instruct people in the uses of various contraceptives, from pills to mechanical devices. All these products are distributed free to men and women workers by the medical compounds of production units, or can be purchased at nominal prices at any pharmacy by those few people who do not work. The big pharmacy in Peking across from the Central Store has an enormous window display about the necessity for contraception, complete with drawings and diagrams illustrating the various methods. Contrary to official statements, contraceptives seem to be distributed to unmarried and married people alike; this was notably the case at the Peking pharmacy. Similarly, free abortion on demand is intended not only for married women: young girls can obtain abortions without much difficulty, though current socialist morality aims at reducing such cases of young, unwed pregnancies to a minimum.

The policy of reducing the growth of the population, or at least maintaining it at a stable level (in recent years it has risen by only 2%) is not demanded on the international level for obvious reasons; but it is energetically carried out within China itself. It is fairly clear that one of the essential functions of the family in China at this time is to allow the government to exercise control over the rate of population growth. In this regard, the emphasis is once more on the educative role of the family, but also on the human relationships that it must foster and develop; no emphasis at all is placed on the family as a reproductive unit. One can even forget reproduction altogether, as this interesting case proves: a man whose wife has just had a hysterectomy is denied a divorce under Article VIII: 'Husband and wife are bound by love. . . .'

If the couple have children, they are obliged to bring them up; but they are not obligated at all to procreate (and adoption is free). Love is thus more important than reproduction; but beyond even love is the supreme sublimation, the effort to build the new society. Deng Yingchao, when she was the wife of the Prime Minister and the central figure in the Federation of Chinese Women, wrote this about the *Marriage Law*:

> Men and women must be encouraged to maintain social relationships, and single people of both sexes to fall in

love with each other . . . It is indispensable to convince (a great many of our cadre) that love and marriage are strictly the private concern of individuals, and nothing has the right to interfere. . . . The harmonious blossoming of love and marriage . . . is the basic condition for a satisfactory social life. However, we refuse to consider love to be the dominant force in our lives, even as we refuse to treat it as a mere amusement. We are, in addition, opposed to all the outer trappings that cannot insure the endurance of love, such as social rank, money, physical appearance, etc.

But the love she means — or at least, love as we had it explained to us — is neither a psychological bond nor a sexual attraction: it is a recognition of moral, political, or professional qualities in the other person, a complicity in common or parallel tasks. Love, it seems, is the possibility of finding the other in a universal code, accepted by the whole society, where 'you' and 'I' have no more reason to exist, since 'we' are in total agreement. Chinese today speak less of 'love' (*aiqing*) than of 'understanding' (*liaojie*). With the Great Leap Forward (in 1958) discussion about the family comes to an end, and is replaced by an exaltation of collective life in the bosom of the working community.

The people's commune is considered to be 'the basic unit of society', the 'microcosm of the communist community', because it is made up of the combined forces of industry, agriculture, commerce, school, and army. The family seems to disappear in this microcosm, all the more so as the Great Leap Forward demands the liberation of new work forces, and a campaign is launched under this pretext to liberate women from their 'household chores'. This truly feminist demand is now considered to have become 'an urgent necessity of socialist production', and, consequently, 'a demand of male members of the society as well'.[1] Thus, it is less a matter of

---

[1] Cf. the article by Guang Feng, 'A Brief consideration of the tremendous historical significance of the People's Communes', in *Zhexue Yanjiu* #5, 1958, trans. by Stuart Schram, *The Permanent Revolution in China*, Mouton 1963.

liberating women, as the Chinese suffragettes and even certain elements in the Jiangxi soviet had wanted, than of liberating the 'female work force'.

> Without the burden of menial family tasks, women can thus play a more positive role in the armies and factories of the society, and help reinforce the spirit of discipline.[1]

Even if excesses of this type have been mitigated by Mao's own affirmation of the necessity for maintaining the family, it is certain that until the present, as I was able to discover during my journey, the theme of women's liberation has been generally understood to mean liberation of women's capacity to join the work force. Only the surface of the anti-Confucian theme of change in the family hierarchy (father/son, husband/wife, etc.) has been scratched; and it will be hard to dig any deeper without directly confronting sexual and psychological issues.

A trend against the family is evident during the Great Leap Forward — but it is altogether different from that at Jiangxi. Since there is a need for women's labour and since nurseries, dining halls, and old age homes can be built, who needs the family? The Chinese Youth Newspaper *Zhongguo Qingnian* (27 Dec. 1958) responds to this line of thought:

> The popular communes are not going to eliminate the family system. They have decided to eliminate the patriarchal system inherited from the past, and to build in its place a unified democratic family.

Mao seems once more to have inspired this moderate response: according to him, the Americans, and notably Dulles, are accusing the popular communes of wanting to abolish the family. However,

> it is important to realize that this patriarchal system long ago ceased to exist in capitalist society. This is a sign of capitalist progress. However, we have gone one step further in establishing a unified, democratic family, which is generally rare in capitalist society. It is only in

---

[1]Feng, 'A Brief Consideration. . . .'

the future, when the socialist revolution will have succeeded in eliminating the capitalist system of one man exploiting another, that it will be possible to make such families the universal rule.

In acknowledging the fact that nurseries, common dining halls, etc., are also inventions of capitalism, Mao points out that their role under socialism is not (yet?) to replace the family, but 'to facilitate the establishment of socialism and the liberation of the human personality'.[1]

We will take the risk of interpreting this declaration in the following way: First, the western patriarchal family is undoubtedly superior to the Chinese patriarchy. Second, the modern western capitalist family represents an objective progression beyond the patriarchy, and the 'unified and democratic' Chinese family has adopted some of its structural elements. Finally, if China attempts to go 'one step further' than the West, the effectiveness of such a step will be proven only after a long period of time, and only if the socialist revolution takes place. In the meantime, the innovations (nurseries, dining halls, etc.) are aimed at liberating personality and integrating it into a supra-familial effort in the general interest of the community, but without in the least undermining the principle of the family itself. Prudence, a retreat from the utopian experimentation of the 1930's, a 'minimal programme' of modest goals: such seems to be the general line, which, in practice, has been variously misinterpreted in both overly collectivist and overly pro-family modes.

The theme of the family is taken up again in 1962, when a Plenum of the Second Committee launches a 'movement for Socialist Education'. A blow against the Great Leap Forward and its tendencies to bury the family in the communes, the movement encourages family relationships, and urges that a battle be undertaken on two fronts: first, in that the State and the communes cannot assume such important tasks as the care of children and old people, the family is called upon to continue to shoulder this economic burden; secondly, and at the same

[1]According to the text of the *Resolution on Problems Concerning the People's Communes* in Renmin Ribao, 10 December 1958.

time, the family must not be allowed to become a cult, and it is important, therefore, that when conflicts arise between parents and children, bourgeois and feudal influences, etc., the family itself become the forum for discussions of class struggle.

An interesting study by Ai-li S. Chin of Chinese popular fiction between 1962-66, based on 232 short stories published in the literary magazine *Renmin Wenxue*,[1] shows the dilemma created at this time by the necessity to reinforce the family for economic reasons, and the tendency to fight against family nepotism for ideological reasons. Of all the short stories, 62 deal with problems between parents and children, 28 with husband-wife relations, and 77 with relations between boys and girls. The fundamental axis, in any case, is centered on ideological preoccupations (economics, politics, ethics discussed on a national scale, etc.) in the relationship between fathers and sons. For the first time since China emerged as a modern nation, the father appears as a positive and authoritative figure (Yan fu) who must be obeyed. In 10 stories the father embodies 'the true line', and serves as an example to his sons. One rather curious thing, which we will discover again in the course of our journey, is that when father and son follow a 'bourgeois' and 'reactionary' line, it is a girl — the son's fiancée — who represents the 'true path'. In 11 stories, not only the other generation, but the other sex or the other family (a young woman 'stranger') embodies the revolutionary cause.

In mother/son relations, the mother is the voice of common sense, but of an emphatically social variety, because she is a productive member of society and places its interests above those of the family. This does not prevent her word from being law around the house: she has a say in the choice of a daughter-in-law and even protests when the son wants to leave the paternal (maternal?) home with his wife. Echoes of the old Confucian family tainted with 'matrilinear' vestiges are found in the father/daughter relations as well: these are authori-

---

[1] Cf. Ai-li S. Chin, 'Family Relations in Modern Chinese Fiction', in M. Freedman, ed., *Family and Kinship in Chinese Society*, Stanford Univ. Press, California, 1970.

tarian, but more affectionate than any other family relationship. Finally, the most strained relationship is that between mother and daughter. Fraught with contradictions between the old ethical values and the emancipation of women, the portrayal of mother/daughter relationships in these stories seems to enlarge on problems which are 'officially' discussed in very little depth. The daughter, for instance, rejects her mother's advice and any interference with her choice of a husband. (Are these problems intensified by those passionate and archaic rivalries between women which, in the West, produce our Electras, who usurp their mothers' roles by murdering them in the names of their fathers? Chinese literature is not explicit here.) The problematic nature of the emancipation of young women also shows up in their relationships with young men. Socially independent and more sexually, politically, and intellectually aware than men of the same generation, young girls must take into account as well the reigning morality in a family that still houses three generations under one roof and easily rejects the symbols of emancipation. Excessive modesty, a long wait before marriage, 'understandings' (*liaojie*) rather than love, but also an exclusivity in emotional relationships (no friendship between 'my' man and 'another' woman) characterize the apparent psychology of the girl depicted in the literature of this period.

*   *   *

It is more difficult to determine — and nearly impossible to define — the role of the family during the Cultural Revolution from 1966 on. The texts are not explicit: one might say schematically that all those matters which were previously taken up by law (Chinese or Socialist) — that is to say, in the broadest sense — now seem to be the domain of 'Communist morality'. Therefore, matters of permanent contradiction, controversy, and ideological choice are dictated by political circumstances. It seems plausible that family bonds have been weakened, if only for two reasons: first, the departure of the 'Red Guards' from their homes and the vast wanderings of young people around the country sparked an explosion of sexual taboos, whereby a certain freedom of mores began to

146

underlie the apparent political austerity; and second, the critique of revisionism frequently gave rise to heated family discussions, with the young people eager to rush forward, undermining the authority of their more conservative parents, who favoured private enterprise and a more or less Liu Shaoqi line of moderation. I will hear more about this later from the old Shanghai working woman Chang Qingmei.

During the Resistance against Japan, Mao had remarked that the Communists would never conquer the enemy without the support of women. The various phases of the social revolution tend to confirm Mao's perception: no given concrete achievement is possible without taking into account the 'revolutionary potential' or the 'work force' of women; and, moreover, without 'raising women to leadership positions'. Constantly affirmed and spectacularly realized at various levels of social and political life — in agriculture, science, industry, education, medicine, within the Party structure itself — the promotion of women to leadership positions still leaves something to be desired. The editorial in *Renmin Ribao* on 8 March 1974 entitled 'May Women Move into Action' declares that:

> As many women cadres as possible must be trained, so that women will be adequately represented in leadership positions at various levels, and play an effective role in the society.

And,

> We must be absolute in our demand that women not be subject to discrimination, to exclusion from any field or profession, indeed, to any form of ill treatment.

Despite the indisputable fact that such directives have, to a great extent, been followed, it was very clear to us that much still needs to be done. For example, in Textile Factory #4 in northwest China, at Xi'an 58% of the 6,380 workers are women. But only 39.7% of the cadres, and only 30% of the technical personnel are women; and there is not a single woman engineer. Another example: because of the current campaign for educational reform, Peking University has a faculty of 2,500 and an enrollment of 3,000 full-time students and 5,000 workers, peasants, and soldiers recruited in 1974 to study part-time: of these, only a third are women. The women cadres we met were generally vice-chairwomen of administrative councils or heads of unions (except in one primary school headed completely by women and in the factory 'The East is Red' at Xi'an, where the revolutionary committee has a vice-chairwoman): rather minor positions, compared to the chairmanship of a Revolutionary Committee or a board of directors. In 'The East is Red,' out of 50 members of the Revolutionary Committee, of whom 17 are permanent, there are two permanent women members and three ordinary women members, plus the vice-chairwoman: a nice step forward, but insufficient with regard to the proportion of female labour in the factory (27.4% females out of 23,000). However, this situation, which the present campaign aims at improving, already implies an immense amount of progress, not only for China but certainly in comparison with the percentage of women holding socially or politically responsible positions in the West as well. Of the 170 members of the Central Committee of the Communist Party elected to the Ninth Congress in 1969, 23 are women: workers, peasants, representatives of national minorities, Party cadres, chairwomen or vice-chairwomen of Revolutionary Committees, one 'red' intellectual from Peking, and, of course, the 'veterans' we've already spoken of — Cai Chang and Deng Yingchao. Only one woman belongs to the Political Bureau of the Chinese Communist Party: Jiang Qing, the third wife of Chairman Mao.

We have come far from the immediate post-liberation period, where one began to call 'the wife of such-and-such a household' or 'the mother of So-and-So' by her proper name. Now, everyone quotes Mao's saying: 'Times have changed, women and men are equal. Whatever men can accomplish, women can as well.' And that is true — as far as it goes. Chinese socialism has given an ideal to the feminine 'self' to such a point that one might well believe that the socialist 'ideal of self' is tailor-made for women. The history of the 'girls of iron' is spectacular in this regard. In 1960, after a long, arduous effort, a worker in the oilfields of Daqing finds the first underground well. He is nicknamed 'Man of Iron'. In 1963, Dazhai (Tatchai), in the central range of the Taihang Mountains, is destroyed by natural disasters. Twenty-three girls from the ages of 14-18, all secondary students, form a disaster team, and, under extreme difficulties, succeed in setting upright — one by one — all the plants in hundreds of acres of fields. They are nicknamed 'girls of iron'. The 'Man of Iron' has found some disciples among young women oil workers as well: in 1970, in the midst of the Cultural Revolution, and after a march on Peking where they were personally greeted by Mao, girls in their early twenties formed the first petroleum extraction team in Daqing: 'We must follow the example of the 'Man of Iron', measure up to the difficulties, and get the wells running before the deadline', declares the team, which undergoes a strenuous period of physical training. The same ideal of physical endurance is found among the numerous teams of women often called 'The Eighth of March Teams', which are in charge of the maintenance of high tension lines in the Pearl River delta area of south China; or in the first fishing boat with a captain and crew composed entirely of young girls on the island of Changze in the Liaoning River in the northeast, etc.

There are no women in the People's Army of China: they serve only in liaison, administrative, or medical capacities. By contrast, the People's Militia does enrol women, and young women in particular. During our travels, however, we did not see a single armed woman in the cities or the countryside; but in any case the number of soldiers we saw altogether was small.

Along with the emphasis on physical endurance, there has been a campaign to encourage intellectual effort: housewives assemble electronic appliances, young peasant women become 'barefoot physicians', women students do advanced research in chemistry and biology. All women devote one hour twice a week to studying the classical works of Marxism, since the days of 'the little red book' have passed and a nationwide effort has been launched to learn Marxist theory from its primary sources. No one could fail to be moved at the sight of these girls and women, who yesterday could neither read nor write, and today are studying *The Critique of the Gotha Programme, The Com-*

149

munist Manifesto, State and Revolution, and even *Materialism and Empiriocriticism* in unabridged versions! We incorrigible westerners are only too anxious to hear them say something new about them: a utopian wish. The problem has not yet reached that stage.

The problem now lies in giving the female population access to the sphere of politics and production by giving women an ideal that can serve as a standard of measurement by which everyone will acknowledge him or herself as a useful, necessary, 'legitimate' member of the society. This 'legitimization' is necessary not only to build socialism, but above all to remove the female body from the polymorphic sexuality in which it takes such banal pleasure, not to speak of the aggressive violence or the psychosis that lies in wait for it. It is only logical that, in a society which has been patriarchal for thousands of years, this 'legitimization' should take the form of obedience to a paternal authority. And, after all, this in itself may prevent the establishment of a modern matriarchal authority, of a 'women's power' which, as far as we can see, would hardly be better than the power of the fathers. So, when I read that a 'girl of iron' navigating her boat is about to lose control of the rudder and herself as well, and old Che comes to her aid and from that time on she submits 'with humility to the old experienced fisherman', I say to myself that if this little story could teach young Chinese women that nothing is everything and that 'female power' does not exist (any more so than 'male power'), this, at last, would be the first step in their own Long March.

Mao seems to voice the same warning when he says:

> I never approved of one's wife becoming the office manager in one's own work unit. Over at Lin Piao's, it is Yeh Ch'ün who manages his office. When the four of them want to ask Lin Piao about anything they have to go through her.[1]

---

[1]Schram, p. 298.

A major aspect of the campaign against Lin Piao centres on his 'cult of the family' and his submissiveness to his wife. Is this the classic mistrust of women? Or is it intended to warn against the seductiveness of power for women?

Traumatized by centuries of 'phallic power', we Westerners have a hard time giving this 'principle' its place, as a simple boundary, a limit, abstract and necessary as a structural element. Either one tends to exalt its peerless, primal, absolute force (on the right), or one denies it in anarchist rage or in the naïveté of humanist spontaneity (on the left). Certain psychoanalysts attempt to persuade us that this element of power (paternal, phallic, symbolic) is the necessary and internal limit of the social animal: since paranoia aspires to power or is aspired to by it, at the edge of that limit paranoia tests the necessary conditions for the existence of a society, and is thus coextensive with the society. However, as soon as one points out that this 'structural element of power' is *politics*, the psychoanalysts shrink back in terror and start talking about 'the sacred' (because there the power is a bit more cloaked?). But how uncomfortable it still feels to say this sort of thing!

This sort of social doublethink may be discovered for what it is more easily in China than elsewhere. The influence of the powerful system of matrilinear descent, and the Confucianism that is so strongly affected by it, can hardly be discounted. These masses may take pleasure in repeating what to our ears sound like clichés; but yesterday they didn't know how to read or write, and today the cliché makes them members of a vast community where they escape their mothers and fathers without disappearing into the idea/abstraction of the Word, since the 'cliché' is made up of gestures, tones, drawings, bodies. . . . These women brandishing paintbrushes, machine guns, and hammers, wearing men's clothing and more and more frequently shouting the orders to men — but surrounded as well by a sweet community of children with relaxed, rounded bodies. . . . Power is politics, and vice-versa: they know it, and women, more than anyone else, apparently long for it; they aspire to it, they identify with it. However, at least up to the present, power doesn't seem to be *established*, bureaucratic, untouchable. Successful cultural revolutions drive it back, badger it, hassle it. Women, aspiring to power, are among the most active in overthrowing it; there are still two sides of this strategy — 'one *yin* victory, one *yang* victory' — that structures the logic of power in People's China. Will this alteration continue? With the help of what line? How much longer will ideology be able to overthrow power and still refuse to speak of the desires that motivate that 'other scene', where, in the family and the bedchamber, those energies that are so easily socialized into tones, gestures, and writing — those energies that are so aggressive when confronted with campaigns, struggles, accusations — rise to the surface and bloom? Or will we witness one day an end to movement, an ossification of power, where the 'female condition' will be no more enviable with women at the head when it was when they were oppressed? More questions from our shore, addressed to the silence of the village square—suspended in time.

For the moment, at least, and despite the majestic Stanislavskian poses affected by women in posters or on stage, the trend does not seem to be toward an establishment of power with the help of women who, as former slaves, would become the new leaders of a new order. Besides, the theatre, the cinema, the opera that presents a heroic ideal in the character of a heroine — not one of the productions we saw had a male hero — portrays women as the catalysts in dramatic situations, or as the oracles of the hidden truths of society, but never as the miraculous agents of success. They initiate, they set in motion a series of events; they suffer, they do not know, they learn; they fail. And then some representative of the Party intervenes, some *deus-ex-machina* who gives the performance a happy ending and validates the efforts of the heroine/pioneer. But (to our eyes at least) he is still a dramatic artifice, and nothing more. Is this a definitive submission to the paternal, political 'ideal of self', 'in power'? Or the continual erection (by this political element) of temporary barriers against the permanent discontent, against the 'not that', the 'not enough' of feminine desire? A guard rail, a door, against which anarchy and the counter-current lean?

In every scene of these productions we find this heroism-mixed-with-weakness. It is disarming, and, consequently, even

152

more desirable than the power that steps in to help it accomplish its goal.

'The Girl with White Hair', by the Xi'an Ballet: A young peasant girl, persecuted by the local lord and tortured by the lord's Confucian mother, flees into the mountains. Her hair turns white from sorrow and solitude, and she is driven to delusions by her suffering and isolation. But at last she finds the revolutionary comrades who triumph over feudalism. This grief-ridden heroine becomes the true champion of the Revolution: the armed militants who seize power for her (and for the people) seem like clever but abstract technicians, agents of an impersonal gesture which she inspires, but does not execute.

'Azalea Mountain' is a *qing chang* (folk) opera we saw at Xi'an. Strained male voices form the chorus: their hoarse lament seems to explode in their throats, with the sheer violence of the effort to spit it out. It is hard to imagine anything more *yang*, accompanied in addition by rigid, staccato movements: legs raised abruptly, slaps, stiff pirouettes. This virile universe is dominated by a weak woman whom it does not accept, because she is sent by the Communist Party. She organizes their discontent, directs their anarchy toward specific, possible, mass-oriented goals. She even protects the *huai dan* — 'rotten eggs — the 'ruffians' who are scorned by men who are themselves the victims of official morality, and act as the unconscious accomplices of the evil laws that oppress them all. So what if the peasant leader is a man? It is a woman who acts as the mind and soul of the combat, as much in prison as on the battlefield. She is the instigator of ruse and realism, and of the bond that makes comrades of the soldiers.

'The Store That Is Headed for the Sun' at the Opera of the Seven Rays at Luoyang: the time is the present, and the style is the anomalous style of the Peking Opera, with its mixture of set poses and delicate gestures from the old concubine opera, toe dancing from the Bolshoi, and exalted expressions with arms thrust toward infinity and thighs snapped abruptly together. Nothing to do with the admirable and well-received *qing chang* of 'Azalea Mountains'. A young girl rebels against her father, who is the owner of a store in the city, and wants to send her to university. Following the ideas of the secretary

153

of the Communist Party, she decides to become a travelling saleswoman in the countryside, and bring the products directly to the consumers. Some *huai dan* try to get in her way, but she is determined to carry out her plans. Alas, she turns out not to be clever enough (i.e. she's a woman); she grows distraught and lets herself be 'had' by the evildoers. Her wagon is overturned, and the heroine is compromised. Slandered by anonymous letters, accused by her father of irresponsibility, deserted by the man who seemed to be her friend (no, he's a comrade seduced by conformity, whom she manages in the end to win over to her side, serving the masses rather than living in the city) the heroine does not justify herself or, indeed, become a heroine, except by the grace of the secretary of the CCP, who discovers the real conspirators.

'Green Pine Mountain' is a film made in 1974 by the Northern Filmmaking Collective. It reproduces the era of Liu Shaoqi, which is currently interpreted as an attempt to restore capitalism by re-instituting 'individual land holding', 'free enterprise', etc. A wealthy peasant disguises himself and attempts to pass himself off as the carter of a brigade. Another peasant — a poor man — becomes suspicious of the evil activities of this 'double-faced' man, and organizes a course of study for young carters. His most active student, a young girl, finally seizes the whip — symbol of power — from the hands of the hypocrite (with the help, of course, of the CP Secretary, a demobilized soldier). But, being rather imprudent, overly confident, and without sufficient strength or cleverness for her new job, she unconsciously allows evildoers to destroy her work: the horse dies, the cart overturns. The poor old carter and the CP Secretary must intervene in order for the cause — which has been launched by the girl's impatience and by her invincible desire for action — to triumph.

The girl — champion of desire, audacity, and revolt against authority. She is responsible for the first stirrings of change, but not for the final success.

A mother or a wife who appears beside her in these productions represents the traditional image of woman: she is either the docile servant of her *huai dan* husband, or the gentle collaborator of her revolutionary husband. She is never the

154

initiator of new ideas, except (like the wife of the *huai dan* in 'Green Pine Mountains') in her failure to get along with her husband. Her 'poor character' is an implicit sign of dissatisfaction and denial — the single traditional form of female expression.

By comparing these 'characters' and their relationships with those in the stories studied by Ai-li Chin from 1962-66, we discover that the wind of the cultural revolution has left its trace. The father is no longer the authoritarian father (*yan fu*) revived from ancient times: the action begins with a revolt against the father and the desire of the young (daughter) not only to leave the family, but to leave the fixed social caste of which the family is part. Moreover, it is not a son, but a daughter, who leads the attack of the real father, by getting a 'symbolic father' (The Party) to support her. No more arguments between women (mother and daughter): the emancipation of the daughter is a political emancipation where she identifies her rebellion (as woman) with the people's discontent with the new bourgeoisie or bureaucracy. No more specifically female dilemma (sex, emotions, marriage) where she might have encountered her mother. No more concern with interpersonal or interfamilial relationships: the sublimation is intense, it taps the impatient desires; but it leaves no room for whatever in the psyche, the libido, the imagination, has not been channelled into political sublimation. As if the family, that harbour of the imagination, had consumed itself; and the desires of the community — represented by the desire of the girl — had vested themselves directly in politics, deeply and fully, but not without failure or drama. If this is not the reality, it is certainly the image that we are offered by the current ideology.

Brecht, the precocious 'Chinese man' of socialism (cf. in his *Mei-ti*, for example) had realized that the failures of the Eastern regimes were not temporary mistakes or faults of such-and-such a personality; rather they were due to the fact that 'something was missing'. For me — having been educated in a 'popular democracy', having benefited from its advantages and been subjected to its censorship, having left it inasmuch as it is possible to leave the world of one's childhood, and prob-

155

ably not without bearing its 'birthmarks' — for me what seems to be 'missing' in the system is, indeed, the stubborn refusal to admit that anything is missing. More concretely, the refusal to admit that social entente, inasmuch as it is possible, is sustained by desire, by eroticism. By a 'negative' that may take the form of a 'manual of the bedchamber', or of the 'sacred'; but which is there at the bottom and which, if ignored, rises to the polished political surface to form the Gulag 'archipater' of China today. There is no 'sacred'; nor is there any talk about desire. One's immediate reaction is, 'let's look for the archipelagos, they must be there somewhere, well-camouflaged under Confucian civility and the elegance of the writings'. The big question, as they say, is precisely that.

Unless, in the arrangement of the Chinese universe, this 'other scene' which in the West gives rise to 'the sacred', 'the erotic' (or, when we ignore it, the 'totalitarian') is constantly present, as an undercurrent imperceptible to us, like Taoism — the subtle but permanent lining of all Chinese life. Taoism, as Maspero has shown[1] was late in becoming a church; and its philosophical system has, from time immemorial, pervaded Chinese life by associating the 'erotic' and 'the sacred' as elements unable to isolate themselves one from the other or define themselves without reference to the other. Will this 'permanent lining' of Chinese socio-political life preserve China from the totalitarian blindness typical of our western rationalism, until, with the help of economic development, a new discursive, familial, feminine and masculine realization of 'what's missing' may be achieved?

---

[1] Cf. *Le Taoisme et les religions Chinoises*, Gallimard, 1971.

VI

Interviews

When a woman does not believe in God, she — like everyone else — validates her existence by believing in man. But whether she anchors her faith in one or the other, it amounts to the same thing. There is only one way out of this 'double bind': to perceive that both 'man' and 'God' are metaphors for unity, cohesion, social continuity — metaphors for language. Thus, when her will becomes so disturbed that she can no longer believe in language or appropriate it for herself, a woman begins to do or write something of her own. An impossible mission, since language *exists*, it remains the same; and for a woman it is more neutralizing and more impressive than for anyone else.

I wish I'd been able, then, to write the *faces* of Chinese women: smooth, placid, closed without hostility, clearly unaware of us in the shadows, the first night in Peking; or looking straight ahead, atop their bicycles; or reflected in the serious cheeks of their children. A fragile, flexible reserve, an unbridgeable distance, punctuated by those blue-grey clothes that mask the body like canvas covers draped over houses in the fear of enemy bombardment. And myself, an eternal stranger, frozen in my thwarted desire to be recognized as one of them, happy when they lost themselves in contemplation of my face and when only my bell-bottomed trousers made the old peasant woman at the Great Wall cry out 'waiguo ren!' (foreign woman). Ill at ease in a group of men. Neither Asian nor European, unrecognized by the women and detached from

157

the men. It was from that uncomfortable position that I had to discover what few truths I could about the direction of their lives at the moment. Perhaps an uncomfortable position, but the only one possible. For after all you know now about Chinese society, you will well understand that it's not worth the trouble to go to China if you're not interested in women, if you don't like them. You will fall ill from incomprehension, or will return home cocksure of having understood it all — but you'll never have crossed the Great Wall; fossilized in your own universe, you'll never have touched the uncertain, hard-to-decipher reality behind the posters and the clichés.

I wish I'd been able to write the *bodies* of Chinese women: full-blown, even buxom, from the effects of age or repeated pregnancies; but always with oval contours, floating, barely touching the ground. Not dancing, but drifting soberly in the early morning air: we saw them, on the day after our arrival, in Tiananmen Square, and on all the roads of the countryside, among the tufts of willow moss that flood the sky in spring. The waistless jackets tied at the neck and the wrists and the wide-legged trousers do not suggest the shape of the body; I can only suppose the narrow, fragile shoulders, the discreet breasts, the robust hips and belly that, with the short, strong thighs firmly joined to the trunk, form the centre of gravity of these creatures who walk so effortlessly. These sinuous arms, these wrists so deft in wielding the paintbrush or the baton, so distracted in stroking the face of a child. These strong, boyish calves, glimpsed when a trouser-leg is accidentally lifted. The body bulges at the knees and the neck, and with the waving of the arms: muscular thighs, flat belly, the skin neither taut nor flaccid, but solid, and immeasurably relaxed, as though their blood flowed with some unvaunted pleasure, as confident and assured as the sleep after passionate lovemaking.

I wish I'd been able to write the *voices* of Chinese women: vibrant, velvety, so low as to be almost inaudible in conversation. They begin in the chest or the belly, but they can suddenly hiss from the throat and rise sharply to the head, strained in aggression or enthusiasm, excited or threatening, when the talk turns to ideology or when the body is on stage before a microphone, as the theatrical tradition demands.

To write these *expressions*, that can slip away unseen: blinded by some nameless opaque pleasure of preoccupation, but also dazzled by an idea that absorbs them completely, snatches them out of the present and hurls them into an infinity where you have no chance of going.

I wish I'd been able to write the *laughter* bursting in the eyes and on the lips of Chinese women. The veil of modesty disappears, and, in its place, a continuous explosion of humour and irony is set off. It is never a bitter, disillusioned laughter; it is at once seductive and serene in the knowledge that seduction is impossible.

I wish I'd been able to write the *families or groups* in the squares, in the parks, in the fields and the factories, where men, with a modesty that can seem frayed and monotonous, gather around women who are equally discrete but far more at ease than they, and mildly dominant; women whose graceful gestures betray an eroticism which no one seems to acknowledge, but which, beyond the political and ideological authority of the day, establishes another authority, more concealed, but perhaps more immutable, and obviously more engaging, since it rules a world previous to politics and is made of archaic desires of which no one speaks, but which are written in gestures and with paintbrushes. A woman in a group is the empty and peaceful centre from which emanate and toward which converge all the actions of the men, destined for work and absorbed in their occupations. Hence the anguished, nostalgic expressions reminiscent of Mediterranean women which I saw — in China — only in the eyes of the men.

'To write' because we lack the necessary distance to risk pronouncing more or less conclusive truths about the life and the development of the Chinese family and the Chinese woman at this particular moment, as we might eventually be able to do when this has become past history. 'To write': to symbolize, with friendship and love, and without pretending to know either the true situation of those you're writing about or the determining factor, the causes, and the trends that motivate us all. But for that one would have had to live with them, become one of them: and even that might not have worked, since, if the need arises, the Joyce or Kafka they will create for themselves will be better than any we can hand to them. Otherwise, I would have had to write the dizziness which, before China or without China, seizes that which is fed up with language, and attempts to escape through it: the abyss of fiction. However, that's not what I felt called upon to do here, where an imaginary 'we' is trying above all to understand what, in the various modes of production, has to do 'with women' — and not only to experience the general impossibility of this plural. Thus, a writing once more deferred. . . .

And so as not to suppress the friendly concern that remains with me, even now, before these faces, bodies, voices, expressions, laughs, gestures of men and women: so as not to erase the disturbing question 'am I different from the tourists who watched the trains go by without knowing who was on them and for which isle of Gulag they were bound?'; so as to leave in suspense, open, and without conclusion this expression of friendship, solidarity, ignorance, and refusal at once that I bring to a China where nothing is finished, where everything is possible — including failure, though it won't be like our failure; including the invention of a new socialism, though it won't be able to serve as an example except in the very long run — here are these themes, here are the faces of these women I scarcely glimpsed.

The Mothers

In the vast tractor factory 'The East is Red' at Xi'an, where 6,700 women are employed, there are twenty rooms designed especially for nursing mothers. Twice a day the mothers stop their work for half an hour and come to nurse their babies, who have been brought from the factory day care centre or, by their grandparents, from home. Away from the noise, in clean and modest surroundings, dozens of mothers keep permanent contact with their children without really separating themselves from their work. These rooms exist in all the factories we have visited, and the goal seems to be to make them available in all places of work.

An infernal noise assaults us in Textile Factory #4 of northwest China, at Xi'an. Cotton dust fills the air and chokes

160

us. With ears and nose stopped up, one doesn't dare open one's mouth. Built between 1954 and 1956, this factory of 6,380 workers has a majority of women (58%) who work, with slight variances from one factory to the next, in more than difficult conditions. The vice-chairwoman of the Revolutionary Committee, Wang Jinchun, tells us that it's not so bad, 'they're used to it', but that there are 'regular medical examinations'; and besides, 'we are doing research into improving the circulation of air and diminishing the noise, until we are in a position to buy better machinery'.

The majority of the women workers are young, and supervised by middle-aged or elderly men. Calm gestures, imperturbable in the fog of cotton and noise. A few eyes look beyond the work — distant, curious. I notice the rounded bellies: the pregnant women are seated in wheelchairs which jut out from among the rows of spinners: they mustn't stand, they mustn't exhaust themselves. A pregnant woman works in the spinning shop until her sixth month; afterwards, she is given lighter work — fabric inspection, accounting, package inspection, etc. A woman is entitled to fifty-six days of paid holiday around the time she gives birth: in case of complications (twins, Caesarian, etc.) the holiday may be extended to 68-80 days, and supplemented by an additional allocation of funds. A woman worker of the second category (that is, the first stage after she has completed her training) earns 38 yuan a month. After years of working and developing skills, one may make it into the eighth category, with 102 yuan per month. On this ladder, most people remain at the bottom: 50-56 yuan. Child care costs only 8 yuan per month, if one leaves the child in the factory kindergarten during the week, or 6 yuan if one takes him home in the evening. The kindergarten in Textile Factory #4 accommodates 800 children from 3 to 6½ years old, cared for by ten teachers and a few nurses; according to the headmistress, it can accommodate more if the parents demand it. The other children are in the care of their grandparents who generally live with the family. When grandparents are available, parents prefer to leave their children at home rather than send them to the kindergarten. Babies under three are cared for in the factory nursery.

161

The children gather around their mother or their monitor with the reserve and the seriousness of adults. Their cheeks full, their expressions solemn, they are always involved in some game where they entertain themselves without excessive noise or activity; the little girls are invariably the winners. They may be smiling, discreet, or ambitious; but I never once saw them cry, seduce, or impose themselves. Little already-autonomous bodies which don't seem, like our children's bodies do, to have been born too early, or to be unable to do without us. An independent micro-society, they show us their games, and leap up to hug us with the joyous cries they have been taught for the occasion. They wave to our cars from afar (one can be only a foreigner if one is in a motorcar); but they also walk arm-in-arm or hand-in-hand, all alone, without adults, along country roads and in the streets of the big cities, long after nightfall. Quickly educated, precociously socialized, they have the dignity of little sages beside parents who, on the contrary, seem like children. They are living examples of the solid uneffusive, and, in some way, anonymous impersonal love of the Chinese mother. One does not kiss, one does not caress, one does not squeeze a child — at least not too much, and certainly not in public. If he is dear to you, he is not the world to you. That he is your desire is indisputable; but he is wary of it. The dignified assurance is more silent, and more easily crushed, in the overly cherished boy; in the girl (whose strong loving father is compensated for by a domineering mother) it is more autonomous, even triumphant. But it seems that the child's personal desire has been marked — I don't hesitate to say 'civilized' — very early on by a social necessity that keeps him subordinate, never absolute. Nobody takes himself for little lord Jesus.

At the Shanghai Hospital, the second annex of the Medical Institute, we were able to see operations performed under acupuncture rather than chemical anesthesia, and one very delicate cataract operation which combined acupuncture with western medicine. The hospital has a gynecology/obstetrics department with 80 beds, where gynecological ailments, especially those due to endocrine troubles, are often treated by the means considered most effective by Chinese medicine:

162

Chinese homeopathy and acupuncture. In a three-bed room there are three women who have just given birth: one saleswoman, one radio factory worker, and one accountant. For the worker, this is the second child. She says: 'This will be the last, so that I can give them enough time and still devote myself to my work. Two daughters — their grandparents will certainly want a boy, but we won't listen to them. The factory paid for me to give birth, but they distribute birth control pills for free as well.' Zhu Chuanfeng has already used them, and will be able to use them again. Still tired, but most radiant of the three, is the awkward Chan Beiyin, the accountant from the north who has returned to Shanghai with her husband, so that she could be near her parents when the baby was born. Many women do the same, sometimes crossing the whole of China; their husbands are also granted paid holidays under such circumstances. It's now been a week since she had her baby by Caesarian section, anaesthetized by acupuncture: 'No pain' she laughs. 'In two days I'll be up on my feet.'

The baby, a boy, is obviously the hero of this story. But she affects a curious detachment when the talk turns to him — modesty or ritual? — and prefers to speak of her work as an accountant, her study of the *Critique of the Gotha Programme*, and of the campaign against Lin and Kong[1], who was 'an eater of women'. It is true that I'm a foreigner, that there is no reason at all to include me in the intimate joys of the family even if they exist, and that I am accompanied by the head of the clinic. And yet the baby still has no name, and his 'christening' is far from the first thing on his mother's mind. She does have one idea, thought: Xiao Di, 'Little Arrow'. And it's not just any little arrow — it comes straight from a poem by Mao, 'Fei Ming Di':

> Vibrant arrows flying
> There has always been so much to do
> Earth and sky in revolution — Time short —
> Ten thousand years too long
> Speed on your way

The baby 'Little Arrow', thus, is borne forth by this extract

---

[1]*Kong*: The Chinese form for Confucius.

from Mao's poem;[1] he is already a whole story his mother has in her eyes, her ears, her hand. In any case, naming him isn't all that important: until the age of seven, he will be more or less a part of herself, or of the nursery, or of the kindergarten — anonymous, an element in the group, protected by his mother or his nurse; and he will be given a name only in order to register for school. Having already been educated by a collective mother, he will be named by the society of adults: fathers and mothers, uncles and aunts. A super — or supra — family?

An Artist

Li Fenglan is Party Secretary for a brigade of 700 people (350 women) in the people's commune *The Bronze Well*, in Huxian. By trade, this 40-year-old peasant is a cotton grower, and works from morning to evening in the fields. A ruddy complexion and rough hands that speak of more than thirty years of hard labour, in all seasons. Quick, intelligent, vivacious — one of those who are communists because they are the most enlightened among the poor. Even if a Party inevitably secretes bureaucrats, so long as there are 'grass roots leaders' like Comrade Li, there is some opportunity for movement within it.

Strange, the moist eyes of this Party Secretary: widening out and then returning within, staring straight ahead, worried, smiling, but anxious behind their smile. She does not look at us, but seems preoccupied, rather, with seeing some inner world, which I cannot penetrate under her calm face, her harmonious features outlined by wind and sun. I am hardly surprised to hear that she is a painter, and to see her work in the exhibit of peasant-painters of this people's commune: 'A Brigade Working in the Cotton Fields', 'Harvest'. The themes are inevitably work themes, and the people — when one can distinguish them in this style where the 'anthopos' yields to a grain of corn, are women. Li Fenglan says that she can paint

---

[1] Reply to Comrade Guo Muoro, in January 1963. Translated from a French version by Phillipe Sollers.

only what she has experienced: 'I don't draw anything that I haven't come into contact with in my work.' And she continues, harassed by my questions, which obviously seem bizarre to her, since I am trying to get her to admit the motives behind her aesthetic leaning. 'In fact, I don't paint the things I see, but I paint them from my dreams, after I've dreamed of them, when I come home from the fields, a bit tired. My dreams are mostly in colour.'

Born a poor peasant, Li Fenglan has learned to read and write rather late, and she has never taken a painting course, let alone one in art history. In the past few years, the commune has organized a painting workshop where specialists come down from the city to teach local amateurs how to handle a paintbrush, how to use colours, how to draw a face, a body, a field. Many peasants participate, and local exhibits are organized: work from one commune is sent to the others, and thus a continually changing exhibit circulates throughout the country. But Li Fenglan has not participated in these courses, and all she knows about 'art' is Mao's discourse on Art and Literature at Yenan. This lack of art education, which is currently carried on according to the social-realism school, perhaps explains the fresh naïveté of her paintings. They seem like the work of an old Taoist artist who dreamed of being Van Gogh and woke up in a people's commune.

Today she is 40, the mother of four children (the oldest a boy of 20). The idea of painting came to her when she was 24 and pregnant with her second child. One night she dreamed of an enormous reservoir of water. Nothing to do with the amniotic fluid — certainly not! But rather with the hydroelectric project in the village, where a dam was being built to block the flow of water so that there would be enough during the dry season. Today Li Fenglan does not consider this painting too important: it is too mechanical a representation of objects.

One must rise above what one sees. Besides, painting helps a woman to better herself. In the old times, women were held in contempt. The idea of a woman peasant-painter was absurd. Now we are happy, but I am happiest when I pick up my paintbrush. I tingle with excitement.

165

When I read the work of Chairman Mao that happens as
well — but in a different way.

Ingenuous words, or learned? We feel ridiculous asking Li
and her fellow painters the subjective motivations of their art:
they refer constantly to the past, to the happiness of the
present, and to the fact that painting is a more direct means
of propaganda than literature for reaching the masses. In any
case, Li is the only one who speaks to us of dreams, of
pleasure in mixing colours: varying yellows, for instance, or
— at the moment — finding different shades of white for her
current project, a painting about cotton picking. She says:
'You can see only a few black dots — the people — and a
vast amount of white space as far as the eye can see, which
must be sculpted.' Comrade Li's husband is a poor peasant as
well; he studied medicine and is now a 'barefoot physician'.

For a woman to be called by her husband's name, or a
child by its father's, is a bureaucratic habit. I couldn't
give it up, but my children certainly won't do the same
once they are married.

In the past year, a group of fourteen women painters has
been working with Li Fenglan. They meet for an hour or two
in the evening to paint together, and work separately as well.
There are few human forms in their paintings: here, two
women lost among a flock of hens larger than they are, on a
green background; there, stalks of chestnut-coloured wheat,
arranged in geometric shapes, the grain larger than the heads
of the harvesters; or trees with reddish leaves that cover the
entire canvas, without perspective, and only a few silhouettes
among the branches. Realism intervenes, but not as it does in
the paintings of the true realist masters of their commune,
who are evidently men, and who paint portraits of the secretary
of the CP. In the women's paintings, realism intervenes to
insert an animal, a bird, or a plant, which is truer than nature
and suddenly seems to become a caricature of itself. Moreover,
sadness, conflict — all that is subject to discontent — is
relegated to caricature as well. The painting, on Chinese paper,
in coloured Chinese ink, in pencil, or in watercolour, is an ode

to serenity, to the calm vision of domesticated nature, where man loses himself in his work, ecstatic, barely discernible. Is it by chance that women are more at ease than men in returning to Chinese pictorial tradition in order to modernize it, and in rejecting the brutal realism which, in any case, continues to assault us, in its posters, like a post-war soviet nightmare?

The Women Intellectuals

The present trend is toward a re-organization of manual labour and intellectual labour, through which the intellectual class would be condemned to disappearance: the only persons exclusively devoted to intellectual pursuit that we were able to find in China were the professors. But the campaign for 'open schools' involves their doing two days of work in the fields or the factories, so that their 'exclusively intellectual' vocation is altogether relative. We must point out straight away that this does not at all signify the suppression of intellectual practice, which, in the division of labour of class societies, has given rise to a caste of intellectuals. If in today's China one doesn't want an 'élite', one *does* want a 'red élite': a term that signifies, on the one hand, that specialists will be politically active and will participate organically in the urgent business of building socialism; and, on the other hand, that their specialization (at least for the vast majority, from whom must be excluded the 'avant-garde scholars', whose education was not neglected even during the reddest years of the Cultural Revolution, whether in biology or in Chomskyian linguistics) will not exceed by too great a margin the technical and scientific abilities demanded of the great masses for the accomplishment of the work in progress. Specialists, yes: but not too specialized; and, in any case, specialists who place political values above scientific values. An intermediate stratum between a society with a rigid division of labour and one where this division will not generate economic, political, or ideological inequalities. That is what seems to be demanded of the 'intellectuals', the political goal for the moment being to eliminate above all a source for new bureaucrats and a new bourgeoisie, which would be fed as much by the tradition of Confucian *literati* as by the still-very-much-present example of the soviet-bourgeois-intellectual-bureaucrat. One strikingly obvious result of this policy is that the general intellectual level has been lowered: education in certain fields and subjects has been restricted, and a considerable amount of the expertise of Confucian- and soviet-schooled specialists has gone to waste. Another all-too-obvious result: the entry into the culture of uneducated masses: 800,000,000 people who certainly know nothing about the subleties of classical culture, but who discuss the *Communist Manifesto;* who have the minimum of technical and hygienic knowledge necessary to the current stage of Chinese socialism, and who write poems and paint pictures the way we dash off a letter.

The best-known current example of a woman intellectual is Bai Qixian. During the Cultural Revolution, when a movement was launched among city schoolchildren to go and work in the country and, thus, align themselves directly with the masses rather than isolating themselves in a literary élite, Bai Qixian was a student in a Normal School. As she recently wrote in an open letter in the *People's Daily,* from her first contact with the peasants, a transformation began to take place within her. But only when her family announced that it was time for her to get married and establish herself in the city 'among her own kind', did Bai Qixian decide to remain in the countryside and marry the peasant Hua Zhenyuan. He is particularly distinguished by the care he provides for sick horses, even and especially at night, when the other men of the village prefer to sleep. A man 'who doesn't speak and who works well', writes Bai Qixian; and this bit of praise — at best ambiguous — is the only thing that's said about the husband during the campaign around the wife. Not only does it leave him in the shadows: it seems, indeed, that the virtue 'few words, no conversation' which Bai so appreciates may be classed among the highest in the Confucian canon which she, by the very fact of her marriage, is fighting against!

The heroine does not see this; but she does perceive other, more salient contradictions, and discusses them with her readers. She comes from a working class background; but, rather than taking pride in having become an intellectual (and exercising this craft, no less useful to the society than any other?), she decides to go to the country. Her father dies of

168

despair; but, by marrying a peasant, Bai Qixian rediscovers her 'humble beginnings': 'We are leaves on a single stem.' Her husband helps her to learn field work, she helps him at night to learn to read. After some time she becomes a teacher in the village secondary school, without giving up her work in the fields. Her husband takes care of the children and does the cooking, which leaves her some time to organize the active political life of her students: a critique of intellectual or other hierarchies, a study of the history of their village, a programme for helping the poor, an analysis of articles on the campaign against Lin and Kong.

"I would like my children to follow in your footsteps'; 'Your letter is a knife in the back of Lin and Kong,' write her readers.[1]

Let us discuss one of the numerous questions raised by this rather spectacular example: the possibility (or impossibility) of 'the couple'. Is it a law that in the dyad that a production unit represents, *one* member must be more or less sacrificed? And if so, what is the advantage of its being one sex rather than the other? No one in China ever spoke to us of 'couples'; less because the problem has been resolved by the idea of recasting the family into the commune (as was more or less suggested during the Great Leap Forward, and as we tend to believe) than because it just doesn't come up; the couple seems to be taken for granted, without any question as to its internal contradictions, other than those inherited from feudalism (the authoritarian husband) or from the bourgeoisie (the 'free morality'). Moreover, not one of the people we interviewed introduced his or her spouse to us, even when we insisted on our desire to meet them. Still the invisible someone (male or female) in the shadows? Do the Chinese, 'structuralists' before the word was invented, consider the *yin* to be always necessary in a two-party alliance? So that modernization could only consist in the possibility, for a woman, to be structurally *yang*, whereas her husband would be content to be structurally *yin*, unless each could be both at once, which would be the ideal? Isn't that what's discovered on the psychiatrist's couch in Paris or London? But that certainly takes us too far away

---

[1] Cf. *Renmin Ribao*, 19 March 1974.

from Chinese consciousness. Since the Chinese have other things to do and don't bother about this anymore, let us remember only these words of Mao on the suicide of Mlle. Zhao in 1919:

> And as soon as the concept of incompatibility between man and wife shall be made plain, the army of revolution against the family will rise up, and a great wave of freedom of marriage and freedom of love will spread over China.[1]

Things are no more utopian today. However, beneath its veneer of naïveté, the austerity of China may conceal, if not more truthfulness, at least certain 'structural imperatives'.

Feng Zhongyun, 53, professor of classical poetry at the University of Peking, finished her studies in 1941; she then became an instructor at Qinghua University and, in 1952, at the University of Peking. An intellectual educated in what's known here as 'the old school', she is doubtless — at least as much as any Western structuralist — acquainted with the prosodic refinements of Chinese poetic genres, and speaks with the pleasure of a connoisseur of the parallelisms, the rhythms, the graphic imagistic representation and the melodic quality inseparable from ancient Chinese verse. However, such things can no longer be the focus of her teaching: Like all instructors, Feng Zhongyun subscribes to the Marxist-Leninist school of thought, which, in her particular field, obligates her to look for 'class attitudes' in literary texts. She is not at all surprised when we ask, 'Do you mean a Marxist interpretation of literature like George Lukacs?'

She answers that she knows some of his writings, but asserts that 'in China today this theory is considered to be revisionist.'

We fear the worst kind of sociologism and the complete disregard for all study of 'form' when Feng Zhongyun tells us that 'the problem is not to replace the study of form, which we used to teach, with the study of content; but rather to find the dialectical relationship between the two. Thus we have

---

[1]Stuart Schram, *Mao Tse-tung*, 1963.

pointed out in class that Li Bai, a well-known Tang poet, writes lines of 6 or 7 feet, which is the canonical form; but when the content is popular, about revolution or discontent, his verse is no longer the usual form, but written in 9-foot lines.' And Feng Zhongyun acknowledges that, certainly, these observations are only superficial, empirical, and that, at the moment, she has not evolved a coherent theory which would take into account the form/content interaction. The research that is being done into these matters in the West is of extreme interest to her, but she does not think that, at this stage, effective changes could be made: 'We have much to learn from western intellectuals, but we must above all invent theories that correspond to the reality of Chinese culture on the one side and the demands of the struggle between the two lines on the other.'

Recently, Feng Zhongyun has taught ancient poetry much less frequently than the ancient language (to a class of 90 students) and genres like opera, the novel, or the essay, where political and ideological problems take priority, according to her, over questions of form: 'without, of course, eliminating them, especially in opera.'

The Department of Chinese still has four divisions: literature, classical language, classical literature, and journalism. In classical literature, the accent is placed on the poet Qu Yuan (of the warring kingdoms) and on the thought of the Legalist School: Xun Zi, Han Fei Zi, Shang Yang. Among the more recent texts, one studies *The Dream of the Red Chamber* and *The Story of the Riverbank*. In the family or love relationships that these novels portray, the teachers attempt to find examples of the class struggles of the era or the revolt against paternal authority, which coincide with the goals of the present *Pi Lin Pi Kong* campaign. An article on *The Dream of the Red Chamber* in the Shanghai University Review (*Xuexi yu Pipan* — Study and Critique), for instance deals with precisely these themes.

If realism is looked for in the novel, the study of opera, according to Feng, raises problems of style: 'Stage performances here have never been realistic, as they have in the West, where you expose your feelings. The problem now, in trying to establish a new art, is how to reconcile this stylized voice, gesture, and meaning with a modern content.'

In modern literature, since 1919, the works of Lu Xun have been promoted. The fundamental theoretical problem in literature has been the creation of a new type of hero.

Feng Zhongyun does not have the impression that any discrimination against women has sneaked into the politics of appointment at the University of Peking, as some visiting American university women have told her is the case in the States. She has been a member of the CCP since 1956; but many young women, party members or not, are named to teaching positions. However, 'as a result of the past', only a third of the students and the professors are women. Married to a professor of political science, she is the mother of two children. Her daughter, after spending three years in the countryside, is finishing her third year of English language and literature at the University of Peking, whereas her son, who is younger, has finished secondary school and is still in the countryside. Ms. Feng believes that this time spent in the country is a good thing: 'Children mature there, and learn the real problems of the nation. This helps them avoid the temptation of becoming a Confucian élite, but it does not keep them from developing the specialized skills worthy of a red élite.'

The fate of higher education remains otherwise open. Feng Zhongyun has spent more time this past year on the revision of literature textbooks than in the classroom; and this revision — dependent on the whole political mechanism of higher education — is far from definitive. A few trends are apparent: to thoroughly discredit the Confucian school; to study the Legalist School; and to critizice the tradition that has glorified Confucius and denegrated the Legalists. The anti-Confucian orientation takes first priority at the moment, even if Feng admits that there is still more to be done: 'The University of Peking used to be headed by revisionists. Now everything must be re-examined.'

Our discussion with the professors at the University of Peking lasted from 9:00 a.m. until 3:00 p.m., with a communal lunch. Feng Zhongyun was the only woman among our hosts. Of all the speeches prepared in advance, where each speaker expounded on the ideological and methodological problems of his or her particular discipline, Feng's was the shortest, the most cautious, and the most precise. Her convictions were probably as strong as those of her colleagues; but she voiced them softly, hesitantly, while her proposals betrayed a consciousness of the limits of her work, and hinted of many questions — for the moment? — left unanswered.

She did not have the assurance of the professor of dialectical materialism, so convinced of his theory; nor the contempt — certainly justified — of the linguistics professor for western linguistics. Her quick eyes — set like a wildcat's above her high cheekbones — closed prudently when our questions deviated from the present line: a sign of some knowledge that's not in fashion today? A sign as well that it's not easy to make us foreigners understand why one may choose to keep silent in the name of a culture that is less refined, but made for all? Outside of public discussion, when she threw herself into the details of the poetry of Li Bai or the stylistic peculiarities of Chinese opera, which 'is never art-for-art's sake, but has its own ideology, its own propaganda', her eyes brightened, her awkward face became more animated, and dimples shone in the cheeks of this serious, knowledgeable woman.

At 35, Wu Xiufen, on the contrary, is entirely the product of socialism. After four years of studying physics at the University, she is presently Professor of Physics at the Upper Normal School of Nanking. A beautiful 'campus' in the style of the old New England colleges, in a huge green park dotted with Ming-style pavillions, it seems more like on imperial city than a university. Specializing in electro-dynamics, it is one of the first schools to have adopted the principle of 'open-door education'. In the teaching of physics, this means that, while they are studying theory, the students apply their knowledge to the nation's industry. Like all normal school students in the world, the students at Nanking know the functional principles of a generator: but unlike the rest, they actually manufacture light electric motors in the physics 'workshops' of their school. These motors are sold to the state, according to state plan. The 'revenue' is certainly modest, since the production is not intensive; but it is consistent, and its educational value is more important than its economic reward. Moreover, one month each semester Wu Xiufen's students work in the factories with the workers of Nanking. The 'open-door education' means, finally, that two half-days per week are devoted to political studies (articles in the *People's Daily*, texts by Mao, and Marxist classics), largely oriented at present toward the *Pi Lin Pi Kong* campaign. After having proven her initiative and her capacity for original thought in this programme combining practice and theory, Wu Xiufen has, in the past two years, been transferred from teaching to the bureau of Educational Reform, where her work is concerned with all fields of study (letters, arts, sciences). She has two children, who are cared for either by their grandparents or at the kindergarten, and she does not seem particularly concerned with women's issues: the promotion of women to leadership positions, the intrusion of domestic life on the intellectual development of women, etc. She smiles, rather like a man, with modesty and discomfort when she is asked what ultimate consequences the campaign against Lin and Kong will have on family life and the status of women; and she answers only with words that are currently prescribed: access for women to political life and positions of leadership, etc. . . . One's personal life is hardly a major preoccupation, 'since more and more men are being re-educated, and helping their wives around the house'.

For every three teachers at the school, one is a woman, and 40% of the students are girls. According to Wu, this is a satisfactory proportion; in the current state of things, there is 'nothing to worry about' as far as women's rights are concerned.

Even more sure of themselves are the women who seem to have the whole compulsory system of education in their hands. We visited the five secondary and nineteen primary schools in the Marco Polo commune near Peking, which send twenty candidates to the University each spring. We also visited the Changjianlu primary school at Nanking, where the directress, Huang Guanglun, told us that teaching has two goals: the first is ideological, governed by the spirit of internationalism and love of country; the second is methodological, encouraging practical skills and physical fitness, according to the theories of Mao. The present system seems to encourage the rapid promotion of young teachers, with special advantages given to women. Thus, at Shanghai University, Ji Ruman, 23, is assistant professor of philosophy, after two years and eight months of studying philosophy rather than the five years required before the Cultural Revolution. The daughter of a family of middle cadres (her father is a research agronomist, her mother a factory worker), she has five sisters and brothers who are all following various courses of study interspersed with periods in the countryside. In this, her first year of teaching, Ji Ruman lacks self-confidence and says she counts a great deal on the assistance of older teachers, both men and women (13 women to 60 men). She is, in fact, less knowledgeable; and she takes little part in the discussion among brilliant historians and philosophers like Fan Shuze and Wang Jingteng, who drew for us the most thorough portrait of the past and the most analytic portrait of the present goals of the *Pi Lin Pi Kong* campaign that we heard anywhere during our stay. When Ji finally dares to take the floor, she points out that there is no real women's organization at the University. In fact, although the *Chinese Women's Association* may well have a big building in Shanghai at its disposal, we did not get the impression that it was currently active, and we were unable to learn anything specific about the activities of this association in Shanghai or anywhere else. The *Women's Federation* seems to have gone to sleep after the Cultural Revolution, and the familial or feminist aspect of the *Pi Lin Pi Kong* campaign has been developed within a new framework — or, rather, *without* a framework, oriented by the directives of the CCP, but left up to local initiative. Like the other women we spoke to, Ji feels that the status of women has risen immeasurably since the Liberation, and even since the beginning of the Cultural Revolution. She, too, sees its greatest advances in the fact that women now have equal rights in work and politics. For all that, however, some vestiges of the past still remain: 'contempt for women among certain classes of people, and not only in the countryside; underestimation of our intellectual abilities, but also of our physical strength.'

In China, there are no 'men's jobs' and 'women's jobs', since women are encouraged to become aeroplane pilots and high tension wire electricians, and since 'whatever a man can do, a woman can also do', as everyone tells us — adding, however, that one must pay attention to female physiology and spare women from hard physical labour as much as possible. Whether by accident or necessity, however, two fields have apparently not been kept by this philosophy from being reserved for women: education and the care and maintenance of the public memory.

Women historians — exhibit planners, researchers, or teachers — provide a symbolic genealogy. Genetic mothers, educators of these masses of peasants and workers who, for the first time in the history of this people (and, in light of the dimensions, for the first time in the history of humanity) are poring over the past. These women awaken and bring into the present the age of politics and ideology from which feudal and capitalist society have kept them apart. To what extent are these women simply the mouthpiece of a programme dictated by the more powerful line of the two that are currently struggling for power? Are they the obedient voices of a memory recreated according to those who are now in control? Or are they formulating a new point of view, contributing to the discovery of a past from which the metaphysics of patriarchal society have kept them apart? A past that can be rediscovered only through a revolution that franchises those oppressed by class and sex? This question as well remains unanswered.

Lu Qiulan is a guide in the Xi'an Historical Museum. One of the richest museums in China, it houses, among other things, enormous rooms full of funerary steles from all periods, including thirteen classical books of Confucianism engraved in stone. She has circled in chalk the passages of Confucius which are currently under criticism in the press. Visitors — peasants, students, workers, soldiers, schoolchildren — stop in dense crowds in front of these books, and read, thus, for the first time 'in the original' the famous precepts ('Live moderately and return to the rituals', 'obedience to the father and to the husband', all the various Confucian virtues) by which they were governed not so long ago, and which Lin Biao is currently accused of having sought to revive in order to mask his aspira-

176

tions to power. Had he succeeded, the power would not have been controlled by an intellectual élite, but rather by a hierarchy of more or less 'intellectual' soldiers and bureaucrats. Lu Qiulan is not at all eager to discuss the present: she insists on the meanings of the Confucian texts, on the social milieu that produced them, the popular rebellions against them. She speaks with enthusiasm of the different calligraphic styles of the past, by which Mao has been inspired. Her work as a historian consists also of advancing research. At the moment, she is working on the period of the warring kingdoms (403-221 B.C.) and the reign of Emperor Qin (221-207 B.C.), when the resistance to Confucianism was at its strongest. She has done extensive research on Wang Chong (A.D. 27-97), who is considered to be an anti-Confucian materialist.

'I am trying to think about his theory against the existence of the soul,' says Lu; and she seems frankly astonished when I ask her if and when she plans to publish her study: 'In China many people work, but very few publish.'

The mother of three children, of whom the eldest is ten, she studied history for four years at the University and has been working at the museum for the past five years. I ask her:

> Wang Chong, for you, is a materialist. What is your definition of a materialist? Wasn't it he who fought against the treatises on the body, and certain Taoist rituals as well? Doesn't the Taoist tradition represent — albeit in mystical form — certain materialist demands against Confucianism?

But my question will remain unanswered, except for her affirmation of 'the complicity between Taoism and Confucianism, two aspects of idealism, both of which are surpassed by Wang Chong'. Surpassed? Or suppressed?

Beside the erudition of Lu, Zhang Shufang, an exhibit planner at the Panpo Museum (where the remains of a primitive commune that dates from 6,000 B.C. are on exhibit) seems self-taught. In fact, she is: thirty years old, the mother of two, she came into the museum as a tour guide. Brushing every day against the vestiges of that ancient society, where women were central figures, she decides to find out more about

177

it. She begins, all by herself, to read Engels on the family, private property, and the State. Then she takes night courses, and attends the lectures given by professors from the University. Zhang has all the enthusiasm of a neophyte: the way she speaks about the imagined life in a matriarchal commune of six thousand years ago makes it sound like a thoroughly recent adventure in which she herself took part. This 'matriarchy' — in which I don't really believe — is transformed, in Zhang Shufang's words, into a modern — if not contemporary — reality. Perhaps because what she calls 'matriarchy' is the desire of 'the other sex' to appropriate time for itself: to enter into the relationships of production and to speak of them, to symbolize them. It's hardly astonishing, then, that the assurance of this young memory-organizer at Panpo may seem insolent, to one who takes himself for a man. That this self-taught historian underestimates, in her passionate naïveté, the 'sexual difference' is, certainly, a lesser evil, compared, for instance, to the classical male oppression of this difference. In any case, to hear her, the matter is quite clear: the wheel is turning, and even if it turns on clichés and uncritical thinking, there's still a chance that it might produce something new.

The Young, The Old, And Love

Zhan Guofei, at twenty, is the vice-chairwoman of the Naval Shipyard Union in Shanghai, an immense enterprise concerned with the repair and construction of gross-tonnage ships which employs 7,000 workers (including 1,400 women) and occupies 460,000 square metres of space, divided among ten workshops. Although it's not an organization of primary importance, especially after the Cultural Revolution, when political, and even managerial, functions were assumed by the Revolutionary Committee, the Union plays an essential role in the organization of daily life. Matters concerning family, marriage, birth, day care, kindergarten, dining halls, death, divorce, contraception — thus, all that concerns women — are regulated by the Union (in conjunction with the Administrative Committee). But the Union also takes care of ideological education: it organizes groups who study the thought of Marx,

178

Engels, Lenin (Stalin is included as well, but they don't study his thought) and Mao; the critique of Lin and Kong; competition in production. It forms new administrative cadres, organizes night schools and leisure activities — sports, theatre, cinema — 'And above all,' says Zhan Guofei, 'it's to the Union that the masses bring their grievances against the management.'

With her pink cheeks, her quick eyes, and her braids, Zhan Guofei certainly does not incarnate authority; rather, she seems to represent what one would call 'the counter-current' — a youthful dynamism, an awareness, a sense of initiative, a readiness to innovate and rebel because she has no status or institution (not even a husband or children etc.) to preserve. All her energy is poured in to 'the cause': meetings, discussions, artistic activities in which, without being 'the star', she participates by giving dance and choral recitals. A sort of fanaticism that has, however, nothing hard or arrogant about it, tempered, as it is, by eternal modesty. What does the struggle against Lin and Kong mean to her?

'Before the campaign, I couldn't ask to do hard labour. Now, thanks to the campaign, I can become an iron worker.' In the ironworks, which are far from the last word in technology, it is boiling hot and the noise is loud enough to burst your eardrums. Our interpreter, Zhao, whom nothing escapes, is quick to tell us that the physiological peculiarities of women are taken into account, and that no one is trying, through an excess of zeal, to transform them from slaves to the home into martyrs to industry. For Zhan Guofei, the problem seems abstract, distant, and confused; she says nothing about it, but shows us, instead, with a great deal of pride, her women friends hidden under helmets, soldering lamp in hand, or suspended in air on the gantries of ships.

One might think that the idealism of young girls, which is one of the essential forces in the anti-bureaucratic current and the economic endeavours of China today, is the public face of sexual sublimation. Zhan lives with her parents, who are workers, and says she knows nothing about contraception: 'They talk a lot about it at the factory, but it's only for married people.' (What she says is contradicted by others.)

After she reaches the age of twenty-five (which is the age that the state currently recomends for women) she will marry someone from another factory: 'because you shouldn't mix work and personal relationships.'

The usual modesty? A kind of puritanism? Or both, combined with a precocious wisdom that is the product of a life 'in society' from early infancy?

'There are lots of chances for young people to meet. They don't hold dances anymore, but people can get together at the cinema or in the parks.'

Indeed, I see them, in the evening, on the banks of Huangpu, holding hands, sitting on the benches, under the arcade of trees, or leaning over the water. I see them as well in each other's arms, disappearing into the dark corners of the parks at nightfall. Tender, discreet, they are silent, or speaking in hushed voices. They never kiss when anyone is watching. The girls — always more solid, more confident, more self-assured than prudish. The boys — a bit frail, childish, slightly effeminate according to our canon. Even if they are not as rigorously chaste as they make themselves out to be, it is possible that their physical relationships consist in the contact of iridescent skin, of sensitive gesture-antennae, of nervous surfaces ever alert to each other's most intricate codes. What they call 'love' does not even allude to this contact, but — rather brutally — signifies 'a common understanding in a common task'. After all, what are our western codes of love, if not narcissistic mirages or — at their most refined — symbolic fusions of two into One, in relation to which those who call Love 'God' are not the most deluded? The Chinese code of love, placing the 'unity' of the two immediately in the sphere of politics and social action, seems crude to us: it deprives them of the troubadours and of Mozart, it leaves no room for the psychological novel or the annual flowering of 'nubile young maidens' in spring. But when our code starts to crumble in Manhattan or on the Berkeley campus — when the body is fed up with its lovely naïveté or its hypocrisy — when it gives rise to 'societies for cutting up men' or to the persecution of homosexuals, what a farce to be nostalgic for the lovesick West on the streets or in the shipyards of Shanghai, where Zhan Guofei is

180

trying — however unwittingly — to sidestep a few hundred years of psychology.

I feel I'm justifiably disturbed, though, when I see the young girl, in love with social struggle, make herself an authority by more or less consciously *using* the father: for example, the young girl who, like all her contemporaries, works in the factory, but who — with the obvious encouragement of her family, and especially of her father, who is a Party member — is preparing herself to become a manager. Or another girl, whom I met in a primary school: the favourite of her intellectual family — doubtless because of her outstanding abilities — she already acts like a little sergeant-at-arms, sure of her own superiority over the others. I know only too well that the regimes of the East knew how to use the love of the daughter for the father to turn the passions of young girls into the most reliable support of a policy which accorded them some advantages in exchange for their blind consent. The game of love for the father has two limits: aphasia and prison. To avoid the one without locking oneself up in the other is certainly our problem. Is it the problem of Chinese women as well?

In the years prior to having children, then: the young female militants, even members of the militia — 'sons of China' — 'heroines of China', as Mao calls them in a poem:

Strong flowers of the wind five-foot rifles
first rays of daylight on the drill field
surprising to think of girls sons of China
preferring battle tunics to red silk dresses

Beyond the essential parenthesis which the child-bearing years are for a woman, we find them again: grandmothers grown suddenly younger, in love with social struggle, passionate, active militants for power or counter-power. A harking back to the archaic mother, who regains her foothold in the family once her son has grown up and her husband has grown old? In any case, this turnabout does not involve the grandmothers with bound feet who stay peacefully at home, take care of the cooking and the grandchildren, and, at most, keep the family's accounts; they don't even have much to say when their husbands, turned Party militants, give them the floor at

181

meetings in the spirit of the *Pi Lin Pi Kong* campaign. These militant women are, for the most part, elderly workers who have managed to survive an existence where all forces seemed to converge against them. Once the threshold has been crossed, they are more at ease with power, more combative, more alert than even their children.

In the working-class neighbourhood of Fangua Long (Perfumed Melon Street) in Shanghai, the people show us the newly constructed high-rise housing project with great pride, and allow us to compare them with the nearby slums, which have been preserved for the education of the young. Here I met Zhang Qingmei, a grandmother, 58 years old. Zhang Qingmei has high cheekbones ('my mother-in-law used to say they weren't Chinese, they came from some minority group') and short greying hair. She lives in a three-room flat with her 93-year-old mother, her 37-year-old son, her daughter-in-law, and four grandchildren. For Zhang Qingmei, life is divided into 'Before' and 'After' the Liberation. Before, she was a worker in a silk-spinning shop, then in a radio factory. She lived in a slum on the same Melon Street where she lives at present: the door was so low one could enter the flat only by stooping down. Her husband died when she was twenty-five years old. From that time on, she was subjected to a 'double-humiliation'.

'I was humiliated by my bosses and by my mother-in-law, who accused me of being responsible for my husband's death, because I have prominent cheekbones.'

Until she was 45, she supplemented her factory income by serving as a wet nurse in order to support her children. The Liberation ends all this: it provides promotion and dignity for women, retirement at 50. A woman who has been humiliated all her life clings to these things body and soul: when the Cultural Revolution breaks out, she attempts to restrain her children, and even joins a 'conservative organization which glorified revisionism: wasn't it true that we had obtained everything during what was called the revisionist period?'

This group of old workers believes itself to be defending Mao and the Revolution. Conflicts erupt at home — 'especially with my son; I didn't want to subordinate myself to his authority, after having spent my whole life under my mother-in-law's thumb.'

Finally, when the young people's movement gains such momentum that even the centralized power acknowledges it, mother Zhang ends up giving in: 'My son was right, but I was following the peoples' word, not his.'

Zhang Qingmei is without a doubt the most voluble person I met in China; she flares up, her cheeks turn red, she leaps up from her bed, and no one — not even the interpreter — manages to stop the flow of her conversation. This energy is not expended solely for the benefit of educating foreigners. Zhang Qingmei is one of the most active retired people in the neighbourhood, most of whom have decided that 'you can retire from work, but not from politics'.

By consequence: not only do these active elderly people preach morality to the young (and allow themselves, at the same time, to be led by them when the waves of the counter-current sweep the country); they also meet every Thursday to discuss Lin and Kong.

'If Lin had succeeded, it would have been a disaster for us women,' she says, with a conviction that ends all argument.

A classic hysteric who follows the lords? So? A suffering as well, which, beside the new lords of China makes itself heard without self-pity. She is active, constructive. An admirable game with power, a role acted out not only for our sake, but to give her a reason to live and to be useful to the community. Parental authority has been stripped of its meaning for this woman, in whose eyes a life without the ancestral powers had been unimaginable. She maintains it only in the irony of her polite words, when I am about to leave: 'Give my regards to your parents.' Her sons have proven to her that one can do without the old, who think they occupy a permanent position. Which doesn't mean that all authority has gone out the window: another authority, more abstract and more stable, has appeared on the scene: the necessity of the movement, as much on the side of power as it is on the side which criticizes it, with a love that knows no other object.

Housewives and Workers

In China, as elsewhere, housewives are the least privileged

among women: I don't mean that they're looked down upon, but, rather, that they seem to be trapped in the old ways more than any other class of women. Not that the *Marriage Law* doesn't give them their rights: on the contrary, it gives them more rights than it does their husbands, as we have seen above. It's not even that they don't benefit from political instruction: in the working-class neighbourhood of Melon Street, in Shanghai, they meet for an hour every Wednesday and Sunday to discuss current politics, but also problems of health, personal hygiene, child rearing. Nor is all their energy drained by the task of bringing up their children: the same neighbourhood, we were told, has a day care centre, which is capable of handling all the children who don't have grandparents to take care of them. A way has even been found to make the housewife useful to society, to take her away from the hearth without making her leave the house. Thus, housewives' workshops have been created in the neighbourhood — subsidiaries, so to speak, of the big city factories. The housewives spend eight hours a day working in them, but are able to go on watching their children and preparing their meals. Mothers, thus, stay at home; but rather than spending their time knitting or chatting with their neighbours, they manufacture coils for electric batteries, for example, as in the workshop of this Shanghai neighbourhood, which is associated with the First Electric Motor Factory. And they earn thirty yen per month, which is of some help to their families. The work is not specialized, and one can generally do it without any training. When the factory needs more complicted work done, it sends down specialists to give the women a few training sessions. Except for invalids, all women under 45 participate.

However, nothing could look less like a factory shop, with its vivacious, curious workers who obviously go about their jobs without giving too much thought to standards and foremen and answer our questions with ease. These housewives' workshops have a stiff, cramped feeling about them; the women are fearful, distrustful, secretive; their eyes evade you, as though you had surprised them at some private, shameful occupation. They speak haltingly, and the trendy theme of the effects of the *Pi Lin Pi Kong* campaign does not seem to excite them. One woman ends up by saying that there are really no family problems, since husbands help with the housework; and, anyway, if conflicts do arise, women are in a good position, because the children are usually on their side and can be used as buffers.

It is true that society makes its selection from childhood, and destines to housework those more fragile women who have not been able to integrate themselves with community. And it is also true that the government is trying to help this 'reject' of social selection to achieve some supra-familial social status and at the same time to take advantage of her unused potential for productive labour. But much still needs to be done: at the moment, these housewives' workshops — frail tentacles reaching from the home to the outside world — are grim, somber places indeed, pale reflections of the political and economic tensions that permeate factory life. Might not the fact that they are staffed entirely by women, without a feminist cause to defend, have something to do with this morose atmosphere?

Among working women, age seems to play a decisive role in determining the degree of commitment to the ideological, political, and economic struggle. The young girls and the older women seemed to me to be the most active, both as leaders and as critics. Mothers, on the contrary — with the exception of technical or political cadres — seemed withdrawn, as though they were listening to the insides of their bodies. They have little enthusiasm for talk. A sign — if anyone still needs convincing — that the classical condition of women — sexuality, pregnancy, childbirth, relationships with the family, housework — is not a primary topic of discussion today. At the very most, an appeal is made to their productive functions, even their leadership capacity—i.e. they are urged to become active in political and economic life. But an in-depth ideological discussion of the family and its inter-sexual and inter-personal relationships is still to be desired. When it comes to women and the family, the quantitative takes precedence over the qualitative; but the qualitative has risen to the surface once or twice, during the 4 May Movement and the period of the Jiangxi Soviet.

185

As far as peasant women are concerned, immense efforts have been undertaken to liberate them from family traditions and superstition. The *Marriage Law* resolved the legal problems and destroyed the clans that bought and sold daughters; the campaign launched by the Cultural Revolution to send young people to the countryside, and the cultural changes which that implies, has not only created obvious bonds between youth and the masses, but has modernized the villages as well. In the Marco Polo People's Commune near Peking, I met young peasant women who belong to an art/propaganda group, read Mao (and a few novels whose titles they can't remember), and write poetry on the political themes of the day. Mothers also participate in this active collective politicized life: there are three cinemas in the commune, and an evening course in reading and writing and political instruction. Xu Jin, who wakes up every morning at 5.30 and works from 6 a.m. to 7 p.m., with four breaks (breakfast, 10 a.m., lunch, 4 p.m.), is happy with her life: her house has running water and electricty, her husband works at the brick factory, her daughters are studying to be secretaries. They don't have Sundays off, but the women work only 26 days per month, and the men, 28; all of which brings in 2,500 yen per year, of which they are able to save 700. Peasants seem to worry about economics more than anything else: the most ancient and common of peasant traditions. As a result, the *Pi Lin Pi Kong* campaign is slow to penetrate *de facto* in the countryside. One even sees women cadres acting like obedient servants before the chairman of the commune. The ideological spokesperson of a commune near Nanking explains to us that the greater ideological work consists in the struggle against superstition, which means: 'Women don't want to stop having children until they've had a boy. Some men still demand a dowry; ancestors are still worshipped on New Year's, at births, at marriages, at deaths.'

Women in Management

Headmistresses of schools (of course); managers of working-class housing projects (obviously), of factories (less obviously): they assume command with calm and assurance. Their stories of gains and prospects, of the failure and success of their schools, their housing projects, their factories, unravel with ease and precision, as though they were merely reciting a series of details that could hardly be otherwise. They are so different from their male counterparts, who get carried away, branding the past with infamy, and turn purple talking about the contradictions in local government risen to the surface during the recent campaign against Lin and Kong. The women managers don't break their precision and their conciseness except to turn the conversation to lighter topics when our questions get too intimate for their taste. (Thus did a headmistress, when we asked her whether there were differences in scholastic performances between boys and girls, when it was obvious to us that the girls were ahead; and a factory manager when I asked her what she thought of Marx's ideas — but also those of certain Chinese Communists of the past — on the disappearance of the family). A humour shines in their faces, their gestures, but is left unspoken. And then they grow serious again, as if they were conscious of being the most responsible elements in the nation, and of knowing better than anyone that this responsibility carries weight and limitations: no escape, no utopia, nothing funny about it at all. That's how it is and they're there to make sure nothing gets out of hand.

Cao Fengchu, 40, is the mother of three children who, having finished their secondary educations, are now working in the factories or in the countryside. A housewife without any particular skills, she has worked in one of these sad housewives' workshops since 1958, the time of the Great Leap Forward. In 1963, she was elected chairwoman of the Revolutionary Committee of a working-class neighbourhood in Shanghai whose inhabitants pay a monthly rent of only 10p (18 cents) per square metre. She has in her charge 35 buildings with 7,000 inhabitants in 1,800 households; the majority are factory workers, but there are also a few doctors, teachers, and blue-collar employees. In addition, there are day-care centres, a primary school, shops, two beauty salons, a bookstore, and a bank. Flashing her teeth in a broad, continuous grin, Cao Fengchu speaks, with an imperturbable calm that doesn't seem to go with her expression of the difficult lives of the

187

people who lived in this neighbourhood before the housing project was built: refugees, beggars, victims of Japanese bombings, rifling through the rubbish bins to find something to eat, without drinking water, threatened, chased, sleeping outdoors or in shanty towns. What has changed?

'Life is stable now.' Cao has used the word that has been uppermost in the minds of all women cadres or leaders past the age of 40 — whether or not they have said so. It contrasts strongly with the image we have over here of a China thrown off balance by the Cultural Revolution, an exalted, romantic, adventurous China. This accelerated rhythm doubtless falls into more or less regular cycles, with the launching of various campaigns; and it seems that the one against Lin and Kong which we are living through at the moment either has not been properly launched, or else consists precisely in stabilizing and giving depth to what already exists, rather than violently overthrowing it. It seems, however, that whatever the style of the campaign, the 'women leaders', flanked by the feverish impatience of the young girls and the grandmothers, are the veritable incarnations of stability; with their acute sense of the functioning of power, they are strength and sustenance of the movement. 'It's not because of poverty that the people are forever suffering; it's a question of power,' says Cao Fengchu.

And what of women? 'We've left our kitchens and our children. One little street in our housing project is called Emancipation Lane.'

The children who play in the streets all seem to know her; they stop their games to greet her, or leap into her arms. She's Aunt Cao, a sort of collective mother, to whom one addresses all questions of housing, leisure, child-rearing, retirement, current cultural and political activities, and contraception.

At the Changjianlu Primary School in Nanking, the administrative staff is composed entirely of women: the assistant director (but there's no director — we were often introduced to an 'assistant' — or a 'vice' — without there being a 'real' chairperson or director) is Huang Guanglan and the Revolutionary Committee chairwoman is Chang Guan. They

188

have in their charge 900 students, thirty-six teachers and an infant school with four classes and 100 children.

Huang Guanglan believes that teaching in her field, mathematics, is too abstract and irrelevant to the daily lives of her young students, aged 7 to 12. She has designed a programme where courses are taught by factory accountants, who train the students in actual practical situations, teaching them the cost of merchandise, the proper way to make out an invoice, etc. Along with this combination of theory and practice, the educational reforms take physical fitness more into account than ever before: regular health examinations, lots of sports and games. Three-fourths of the classes we visited were in the process of playing games involved with muscular dexterity designed to help them grasp some mathematical or anatomical subtlety. We were particularly impressed with the system of eye exercises, where tradition meets modern medicine to help the little scribes, who must learn the whole basic written vocabulary in two years.

Calm, practical application, and a sense of play: these are certainly instructions from 'higher up' which follow the 7 May directives of Chairman Mao on the relationship between studies and 'other kinds of knowledge'. But all these instructions are extremely generalized; they stir up a good deal of enthusiasm, certainly, but it is impossible to apply them to concrete circumstances without individual initiative. Therefore, the headmistresses — with their self-assured modesty and their matter-of-factness — seem to be the true creators of the new 'open school'.

Our meeting with the managers of the Shanghai Naval Shipyard (7,000 workers, including 1,400 women; ten workshops in 460,000 square metres) was presided over by a woman: this fact is worthy of note because it was the single such experience we had during our journey, except for a visit to the Xi'an Tractor Factory. Sun Zhaofeng, still in her forties, the cadre of the administrative office, was responsible for explaining to us the effect of the current political trends on the shipyards. In the printing shops of the Xinhua agency in Peking we had already heard the young chairman of the Revolutionary Committee, Zhang Hongxie, give a scathing exposé of Lin's

189

right-wing leanings: the most important objective of the current campaign, according to him, was to 'get rid of the cult of personality' and to 'get rid of nationalism, in favour of internationalism'. Was this interpretation going to be confirmed here? With the reassuring calm of a 'leader', full of information but oddly uninhibited by it, Sun Zhaofeng managed to establish an equilibrium: Lin's right-wing leanings are obvious; he wanted to reverse the direction of the Party, seize power, and go backwards, towards capitalism and the false humanist morality of Kong. But what's even more disturbing for the shipyards, she says, is that Lin called himself — and indeed was — a leftist. No one anywhere in China told us that Lin Biao had leftist tendencies. One rightist word and he's over the fence; and even if, as we foreigners think, he does seem 'leftist', that's no more than an appearance, that must be seen through, to get straight to the 'essence'. For Comrade Sun, on the contrary, there is a good deal of leftism in the Lin Biaoists of the shipyards: 'For instance, they may want to build 400,000 ton ships, which would be impossible: it goes way beyond our capacity, and assumes we have the potential of a European shipyard. In fact, this excess of zeal results in our building nothing at all. This ultra-leftist line showed up during the Cultural Revolution.'

'Are you saying now that the people are growing more realistic,' we ask, smelling 'economism'.

'No,' answers Sun Zhaofeng, without hesitation. 'More materialistic.'

'So' — in our distrust, we can't stop asking for clarification — 'why do you say that Lin was a Confucian who preached the "invariable medium" since he was, rather, a "leftist"?'

'The Invariable Medium means ignoring contradictions. Kong ignores them by preaching "virtue", Lin by idealizing "work".'

Sun Zhaofeng is visibly a proponent of the permanent confrontation between the two lines, where neither one gains so much ground as to freeze the situation into a 'Golden Mean', without profit or development. For production to continue, there is certainly a need for local initiative to compensate for the still rather primitive technical capacities of the yards:

The technicians said that a stock of 3,000 tons would not hold a 10,000 ton ship. The workers protested; the Revolutionary Committee supported them and conducted a study which proved that the workers' proposal was within the limits of possibility. Therefore, you see, it's neither a matter of giving in every time to the demands of impatient workers and leftists, nor of continually submitting to the prudence of cadres and technicians.

Against the 'Invariable Medium' — innovation without too much hurry, Comrade Sun is there to insure, along with others — more than some others — the limits of the possible.

Thirty-two years old, an assembly worker at the tractor factory *The East is Red* at Xi'an, Wu Beijin became assistant chairwoman of the Revolutionary Committee during the Cultural Revolution. The factory has 23,000 workers, including 6,700 women, and its story is typical of the Chinese complaints about Russian technical assistance. Slow, too costly, and not sufficiently specialized, negligent in training Chinese specialists, and interrupted in the process, 'Soviet aid' is the principal villain in the drama of socialist reconstruction that has been a frequent refrain in China, and particularly in this dark, gloomy factory.

Wu Beijin, with two children and a husband who was formerly a labourer and now a technician, considers herself a happy wife and mother: 'He is proud that I'm a political leader, and I'm proud that he knows the trade better than I do.'

She is one of the highest-paid workers in the factory, earning 240 yuan per month, six times as much as the worker on the bottom of the scale and four times more than the majority of women workers. Her intelligence, her ease in assuming responsibility, are certainly worth paying for, much more so since no one in China seems to believe in the egalitarian society we imagine from this side, looking at all those identical blue uniforms. Wu Beijin is the only one who spoke of a 'woman's problem', not as a factor in the development of Chinese economy, nor even as an issue in the *Pi Lin Pi Kong* campaign, but as a problem concerning the entire world:

We know that, on a worldwide scale, women are struggling on many fronts. We aren't aware of all the aspects of the struggle, but it is certain that by uniting we will make things happen a good deal faster. Obviously, it won't be easy to get along — our traditions and our problems are all so different.

It seems as though national centralized activities concerning women have been suspended for the moment: the magazine *Women of China,* on whose covers Mao's own drawings frequently appeared during the Cultural Revolution, has gone out of print. Even if the *Federation of Chinese Women* exists on a national scale, with *Women's Associations* for the provinces and municipal offices in the cities, it seems from what Wu Beijin says that all the activity carried out by the Party with regard to women happens locally, in individual factories, led by a special section of the union. Courses are organized for women where they learn the foundations of political theory or receive the technical training necessary to qualify for their jobs: these courses generally include men as well, but courses in hygiene and contraception are designed for women alone, as are political meetings where an attempt is made to understand the concrete consequences that political and philosophical texts currently circulating in the nation will have on women. 'That allows women to change and grow. Now that women are leaving their homes and earning as much as men in the factories, it's important for them to pick up their paintbrushes and move to the front lines.' 'To pick up their paintbrushes' means, for Wu Beijin, to become cadres or activists: as we say, 'to take the floor', meaning to participate in the political structure and its counter-current. It is an ideological goal which will take time to achieve. Poised, always realistic, Wu Beijin believes that there are many structural and economic questions that must be resolved as well: this will, no doubt, also serve to 'raise women's consciousness'.

As Deng Xiaoping, our UN Representative, said, we are in the 'third world', a backward country, in other words. In certain factory shops the work is much too hard; we must make it easier with the means at hand. In 1973

192

more than 1,000 technical reforms proposed by workers and technicians to better working conditions went into effect. A department was created to insure the workers' safety. The workers must undergo regular physical examinations. An extra 600,000 yuan was allocated to buy new uniforms. We are trying to minimize the heat, the noise, and the monotony of the work. For example, a worker does not specialize in one machine, but must learn how to operate several. We avoid machine-belt labour: it diminishes incentive, and, thus, efficiency.

She is speaking as one responsible for the health, equilibrium, and lives of 23,000 workers — men and women. Is she man or woman? At a certain point in her report she feels justified in forgetting the difference.

The campaigns have their women leaders as well: their conversation is less brilliant, their manner less assured; they are, at times, even self-effacing before the male *chai* men, to whom they leave the last word. But their biographies are certainly more dramatic. An intense life-experience has thrust them from a patriarchal world which hadn't moved for millenia into a modern universe where they are called upon to command. It is that which gives them their air of timelessness, of almost lethargic detachment, which surpasses the fixed realism of women in cities.

Mme. He Lixian belongs to the Revolutionary Committee of the *Bronze Well* people's commune in Nanking, at the mouth of the Yangze River. The chief occupation of this commune of 30,000 people is forestry; but they also grow grains and vegetables. He Lixian's parents were poor peasants who, at certain times of the year, were forced to go begging in order to feed their children. Driven by misery, they ended up selling Lixian's youngest brother and sister, and 'engaging' He Lixian to a young man when she was fourteen. An 'engagement' which, in 1949, before the *Marriage Law*, was tantamount to the sale of child labour. Her fiancé, a few years older than herself, didn't expect a wife out of the bargain; but that didn't prevent He Lixian from living in the ambiguous status of potential wife and farm-worker until the engagement was broken off by the enforcement of the *Marriage Law* in all the villages of the country. At twenty-two, she married a comrade of her choice; they now have two children. He Lixian is happy to show us the commune's latest acquisitions for women's health care: a hospital with a section for gynæcological and prenatal examinations and a section for difficult deliveries (ordinary deliveries are handled by the medical stations in each brigade). But this unwilling-fiancée-turned-political-leader does not like to confine herself to female concerns: the typical modesty is amplified by bitter personal experience, and probably she feels it's better not to talk about all that, but to transcend illness and childbirth and worry about increasing production and eliminating superstition. For the rest . . .

> Giving birth was a painful, and often catastrophic, affair in the villages in the old days. Now we are medically prepared to eliminate practically 100% of the risks. Obviously, for women, for myself, there's a certain glory in giving birth, it raises your status particularly in the eyes of the parents-in-law. Whether that's still a superstition, I don't know. In any case, we always find vestiges of the past around these family events: wedding or birth celebrations. And many women don't even think about family planning until after they've had a son.

He Lixian is against all that, for primarily economic reasons:

> Chairman Mao said that we must devote everything to defence and production. Superstitions lead to waste.

Her realism quickly leads to hardness, to ostracism. The heavy tradition visibly weighs on those who are fighting it, by giving them, especially in the countryside, an orthodoxy even more severe than that contained in the generally dialectical instructions of the *People's Daily* — not to mention the recent relaxed and humorous speeches of Mao himself. Relief might come from a complete change in the style of economic administration and propaganda — but it's hard to determine *which* style would overthrow the tradition more quickly, more efficiently, and without creating new social and ideological inequalities. It's hard to see how the policies of the Jiangxi

Soviet, which are more attractive to us, could be applied to a state of 800,000,000 people; for a long time to come the countryside will still be the place where the 'struggle between the two lines' will lean to the side of stabilized power — of economism, if not bureaucracy.

At school, in the factories, in the countryside — women administrators are the conscientious guardians of stability, of the limits of the possible. They form a sort of rational centre, an 'invariable measure', if not an 'Invariable Medium' in this nation where movement alternates with harmony.

It is, paradoxically, a volleyball game in the magnificent Peking Stadium that best sums up the character of Chinese women in posts of command. A match between Chinese and Iranian women: the Chinese women, with lithe, slender, athletic bodies, looking rather like skinny boys, silent, placid, precise, passing the ball or sending it over the net as if they were playing chess, but without the pained concentration of a Botvinik or a Fischer — a bit careless, a bit dreamy. The Iranian women, clearly more corpulent, hair in the wind, passionate, highly excited, hugging and kissing each other after each success, piercing the air with their shrill cries, which at first worried, then amused the Sunday crowd on the eve of May Day. In short, the Cartesians versus the Bacchantes. Needless to say, the Cartesians ran away with the game: 15-9, 15-9, 15-5. Needless as well to say that the Chinese boys — more frail, more adolescent — were beaten by the Iranian boys, real 'machos', territorial lords. Certainly I tend to exaggerate the symbolic importance of this encounter, which I just happened to see because I was there at the moment and because the Chinese had decided to participate in the Olympics. But I can't help seeing a symptom there: the world of phallic supremacy, our Indo-European, monotheistic world, is still obviously in the lead. But if we take men and women together, here and in China, the co-efficient of ability, shrewdness — and, let us say — intelligence will be higher on the side of the Chinese. And this, because of Chinese women; because, after all, of the little 'difference/resemblance' (as ancient Chinese logicians would say) between the two sexes in China.

195

VII

To Risk a Renaissance

When the hare and its companion
Race across the dale
Who can say, 'The female's this
And that one is the male?'
                              — Chinese folk song

Fire marries gold, gold marries man.

                              —Chinese proverb

How far have I come, then, after this journey, from the silence in Huxian Square?

Often I have the impression that the problems of Chinese women, arising as they do from feudalism and Confucianism, have nothing to do with ours, which are cornered between monotheism and capitalism. What do we have to find in this matrilinear descent, this 'mother at the centre', this Confucian family with its oppressed and voiceless wife who is nonetheless a powerful force in the bedroom, before the carved tablets of the dead, and, in her old age, in the family itself? What relation is there between our women saints and revolutionaries and these women with bound feet, these concubines, these Taoist warriors? What is there in common between the girl in Boston who extracts her menstrual blood with a syringe and the girl in a blue shirt who wants to become an ironworker under the portrait of Mao and gives her maiden name to her child?

At times I feel as if the reactions are the same: the need to be legitimized by a paternal function, the impossible relationship between mother and daughter, the suicidal appeal of a polymorphic sexuality in the face of the crumbling social order: the harmony with ancient rhythms, sounds, and colours that either precedes logical abstract systems or intersects them.

When a woman here tries to draw attention to herself, she can choose one of two ways: either she can identify herself with the power (and make masculine demands 'to do what men do') or she can cast herself as an outsider (as a rebel or as a mute, sick body, according to her capacity to see her 'difference' as dialectical to the accepted order of things). Masculine demands, more common in the United States than in France, are exciting at first; they grow disturbing if one takes the trouble to think that they cast the man as the 'bad guy' and, consequently, condemn the woman to isolation, or to the sad state of having an inferior mate, if the form (couples, families) persists. Thus, in an effort to maintain the equilibrium, the most lucid women believe that the sexual difference must be preserved: to insure desire between the two sexes, even if that desire is based on other foundations. But which? That remains to be seen.

But who tells us that this generous, psychoanalytically reinforced maintenance of our sexual difference does not arise from an outdated concept of society: a concept based on the couple, the Family, the Father, the Man? Certainly, if the death of man is proclaimed after the death of God — by, among others, the women's movement — we may find ourselves wallowing about for a time in the mediocre little perversion of consumer society while awaiting the violent revenge of the fathers; but before, perhaps, discovering — if it's not already too late — that neither man nor woman exists, and that neither one needs the other. Before discovering that any individual must maintain himself in relation to an abstract instance — symbolic if you like — that's not necessarily his sexual partner, nor even his psychoanalyst, nor his Party — but a *social practice*: political, aesthetic, scientific. What if the current rage of women against Man, against society, were only a passageway, an incidental feature on the road toward such a discovery, the last anthropological vestige we have to face? Television has just impressed us with the urgency of enforcing

197

planned population control, if humanity is to survive another hundred years. Thus — if you didn't already guess — the pill wasn't invented just for fun. But then what are you going to do with a woman who's not a mother? You've got to figure it all out, quickly — hurry up, Minister of Women or what have you — there's no time to lose. . . .

And anyway, why not? But if a woman can't find her human worth in motherhood any more — if we don't even *ask* her to be a mother any more — doesn't this reversal of the social demand imply as well that the privileged relationship of the daughter to her father should be seen in its *symbolic* (rather than *reproductive*) aspect? and should be actualized in the more or less important works of the community? Women would no longer be baby machines: but, with this hollow fragile, symptom-ridden body, would they become the last pillars of a society that has been corroded by the crisis of the nineteenth century, at least in the West? Before going through their own sort of identity crisis, which will be the veritable revolution of industrialized society, delivered of the anguish of production and procreation: neither man nor woman nor uni-sex: a whirlwind of laughter and collision. . . .

The women in China are so similar to the men: these Chinese women whose ancestresses knew the secrets of the bedchamber better than anyone, and who are so sober and serious today, under their grey-blue uniforms. . . . Whose austerity is relaxed in their paintings, before their exhibits, or in the arms of their children (no more than two, according to family planning) . . . the pill in their pockets. . . . One could say that they 'censure sexual differences' and ascribe it to their past or to the ignorance that *our* well-known prototypes — from Electra to the suffragettes — manifest in this regard. . . . But suppose this reproach — insofar as it is a reproach — could only make sense in our paternally dominated framework, where we have lost all trace of a 'mother at the centre'? If, in China, a tradition — so long as one managed to free it from its hierarchical-bureaucratic-patriarchal burden — made it possible that (aside from the *anatomical*) there would be no more *symbolic* difference between two metaphysical entities (men and women) — but rather a subtle

198

differentiation on each side of the biological barrier, which itself would be recognized by a social law only to be contested again and again.

If, to exist as such, every society needs to assume, if not to recognize, the symbolic paternal function (not the real daddy, but a taboo, a law, a structure), then in China, because the society bears active traces of two familial models (matrilinear and patrilinear) this function is *assumed by women as well.* This allows them, even when the demand of social and economic development oppress them to the point of slavery or martyrdom, to function as the most solid support of the social order, of its administration, of its reform, and even of its revolution. In short, it gives them a way of functioning that is not all that different, in its social effect, from that of the Chinese men, of the real father — since he sees himself, consequently, deprived of absolute possession of the *yang* and gifted with a good deal of *yin.* When Chinese Communism sets itself to eliminating in its members — male or female — the appetite for consumer goods, the profit motive (economist, or revisionist), it's clear that it is attacking pragmatic, materialistic, psychological tendencies, all considered 'feminine' by patriarchal society. But, by addressing itself thus to women, it appeals to their capacity to assume the symbolic function (the structural constraint, the law of the society): a capacity which itself has a basis in tradition, and which is even more profound, since it includes the world prior to and behind the scenes of Confucianism.

However, a *power* (what I called 'a paternal function' above) assumed (and not *represented*) by a woman is already a power with a body, and a body that knows about power: symbolic contract, economic limits, but also impulse, desire, and contradiction. A power in infinite process: *a power that cannot be represented.*

Thus, when Mao launches women, on the heels of students, into the Cultural Revolution (cf. his calligraphic design, WOMEN OF CHINA, from Autumn 1966) — when women today are placed in posts of command — mightn't it be to proclaim that *power* in a society is not to be abolished (that would be nonsense or poetry in any case, a whole different question) — but, rather, that it must not be represented — and, in fact, cannot be? Neither by a head of state — a prince incarnating the law for feudal imaginations (ah! Hegel); nor by a social contract providing for the functioning of private property interests and the bourgeois development of production (oh! Goddess of Reason, bride of Robespierre, mother of terror); nor by the more or less cold-blooded violence of a party that established its opposition to all 'others' — a negation of the contract, a return of the body repressed in the torture chambers of prison camps (Stalin — and you name the rest).

Nothing is easier than to see them — one of these three forms of power or the three together — in China: isn't Mao easily taken for a feudal lord, Chinese ideology for a flat and restrictive positivism, and the CCP for an offshoot of dogmatism? Indeed, nothing is more obvious. On one condition: that we don't take into account the fact that a society is a complex organism, that its ethic is determined perhaps above all by its family structure, and that it thus depends directly on the economy of the sexual difference. But old Hegel was the last to take that into account: ever since, the 'social sciences', specialized or compartmentalized, have abandoned ethics, and the sexual body has found refuge only in the shadows of psychoanalysis, apart from the concerns of the day. If, by contrast, one paid attention to women, to the family, and to the sexual difference, inasmuch as these factors determine a social ethic, and after having examined their problematic aspects in China, one might realize the necessity for creating a society where power is active, but not symbolized by anyone: no one can appropriate it for himself if no one — not even women — can be excluded from it. Women, the last of the slaves, necessary for the maintenance of their masters' power; their separation from power insures that power remains representable, and that it is up to men — fathers, lawmakers — to represent it.

A power, thus, represented by none, not even women, but recognized by all, and assumed and exercised by each: man and woman, men and women, exercising it only to criticize it, badger it, force it to move. This would explain why the

200

'tribunal' has been replaced in China by 'People's Assemblies': there would be no more *instance* of the law in itself, if each individual, man and woman, took it upon himself to remake it by permanently confronting it with his/her practice, in his/her discussions with others, in each individual act, in each concrete moment. A utopia? An eventuality, a subject for dreams of the future, while in the present nothing has been able to surpass the rational rigour of bourgeois law and its concurrent ethic? An eventuality even so, since our system is cracking, and over there another is trying to establish itself, taking off from another tradition and with other preconceptions?

Many Chinese phenomena which we have discussed here keep us from believing this hypothesis, and prompt us to think, rather, that the Chinese are still passing through a period of transition, if not failure, where certain freedoms will be bought at the very high price of censuring certain others. Other phenomena lead us to believe that the die is cast, in China, for a socialism without God or Man, which will accompany, at a distance, the perilous, unprecedented renaissance of a new humanity that is gathering momentum here.

BIBLIOGRAPHY

The following books are suggested for those who wish to pursue these matters further:

BROYELLE Claudie, *La Moitié du Ciel*, Denoel Gonthier Ed. 1973.

FREEDMAN Maurice, *Lineage Organization in Southeastern China*, London, School of Economics Monographs on Social Anthropology, 18.

FREEDMAN Maurice, *Chinese Lineage and Society*: Fukien and Kwangtung, London, School of Economics Monographs on Social Anthropology, 33.

FREEDMAN Maurice (editor), *Family and Kinship in Chinese Society*, Stanford Univ. Press, California, 1970.

GRANET Marcel, *La Civilisation chinoise*, Albin Michel, 1929 (1968).

GRANET Marcel, *La Pensée Chinoise*, Albin Michel, 1934.

GULIK Robert van, *La vie sexuelle dans la Chine ancienne*, Gallimard, 1971.

HSU Francis L. K., *Under the Ancestor's Shadow*, New York, Columbia Univ. Press, 1948.

MARGOULIES Georges, *Le Kouwen chinois*, selected texts with an introduction and notes, Paul Geuthner, 1926.

MASPERO Henri, Taoism and Chinese Religions, Gallimard, 1971.

MEIJER, M. J., *Marriage Law and Policy in the Chinese People's Republic*, Hong Kong Univ. Press, 1971.

NEEDHAM Joseph, *Sciences and Civilization in China*, Cambridge.

SCHRAM Stuart, *Mao Tse-Tung*, 1963.

SCHRAM Stuart (editor), *Mao Tse-tung Unrehearsed*, talks and letters: 1956-1971, Pelican Books, 1974.

SNOW Helen, *Women in Modern China*, Mouton, 1967.

YOUNG Marilyn B. (ed.), *Women in China*, Michigan Papers in Chinese Studies, 1973.